Introducing Web Development

Jörg Krause

Apress®

Introducing Web Development

Jörg Krause
Berlin, Germany

ISBN-13 (pbk): 978-1-4842-2498-4   ISBN-13 (electronic): 978-1-4842-2499-1
DOI 10.1007/978-1-4842-2499-1

Library of Congress Control Number: 2016961532

Managing Director: Welmoed Spahr
Acquisitions Editor: Louise Corrigan
Development Editor: James Markham
Editorial Board: Steve Anglin, Pramila Balan, Laura Berendson, Aaron Black, Louise Corrigan, Jonathan Gennick, Todd Green, Celestin Suresh John, Nikhil Karkal, Robert Hutchinson, James Markham, Matthew Moodie, Natalie Pao, Gwenan Spearing
Coordinating Editor: Nancy Chen
Copy Editor: Kezia Endsley
Compositor: SPi Global
Indexer: SPi Global
Artist: SPi Global, image courtesy of Freepik.

Distributed to the book trade worldwide by Springer Science+Business Media New York, 233 Spring Street, 6th Floor, New York, NY 10013. Phone 1-800-SPRINGER, fax (201) 348-4505, e-mail orders-ny@springer-sbm.com, or visit www.springer.com. Apress Media, LLC is a California LLC and the sole member (owner) is Springer Science + Business Media Finance Inc (SSBM Finance Inc). SSBM Finance Inc is a **Delaware** corporation.

For information on translations, please e-mail rights@apress.com, or visit www.apress.com.

Apress and friends of ED books may be purchased in bulk for academic, corporate, or promotional use. eBook versions and licenses are also available for most titles. For more information, reference our Special Bulk Sales–eBook Licensing web page at www.apress.com/bulk-sales.

Any source code or other supplementary materials referenced by the author in this text is available to readers at www.apress.com. For detailed information about how to locate your book's source code, go to www.apress.com/source-code/.

Printed on acid-free paper

Contents at a Glance

Contents

About the Author

Jörg Krause has been working with software and software technology since the early 1980s, beginning with a ZX 81 and taking his first steps as a programmer in BASIC and Assembly. He studied Information Technology at Humboldt University, Berlin, but left early, in the 90s, to start his own company. He has worked with Internet technology and software development since the early days when CompuServe and FidoNet dominated. He's been with Microsoft technologies and software since Windows 95.

In 1998, he worked on one of the first commercial e-commerce solutions, and wrote his first book in Germany, *E-Commerce and Online Marketing*, published by Carl Hanser Verlag, Munich. Due to its wide success, he started working as a freelance consultant and author in order to share his experience and knowledge with others. He has written several books for Apress, Hanser, Addison-Wesley, and other major publishers along with several self-published books—a total of over 60 titles. He also publishes articles in magazines and speaks at major conferences in Germany. Currently, Jörg works as an independent consultant, software developer, and author in Berlin.

In his occasional spare time, Jörg enjoys reading thrillers and science fiction novels and going on a round of golf.

Introduction

The Foundation of Web Development

The book describes the basic techniques, protocols, and standards of the web:

- The underlying protocols such as HTTP

- HTML, currently in version HTML5

- CSS, currently in version CSS3

This is a base, independent of platform and environment. With this foundation, you can adapt all the sources on the Internet and read all the documentations you'll need to learn programming the Web.

Who Should Read this Book?

This book is aimed at beginners and web developers who are new to the web world.

In any case, I tried not to ask for prerequisites or conditions of the reader. You do not need to be a computer scientist, nor in perfect command of a language, and you don't need to know rocket science. No matter in what context you have encountered Jade, you will be able to read this text.

What You Should Know

Readers of this series have hardly any requirements. A current operating system is always a good idea. Use either Linux or Windows; it really doesn't matter as long as you install a program and run it. You should have your favorite browser handy. An editor is helpful for some examples, such as Visual Studio Code or Sublime Text. Both work on all operating systems.

How to Read this Book

I will not dictate how you should read this book. In the first draft of the structure, I tried several variations and found that there exists no ideal form. However, readers today tend to consume smaller chunks, independent chapters, and focused content. This book meets this trend by reducing it to a small issue, focused, and with no "blah-blah" for the inflation of the volume.

Beginners should read the text as a narrative from the first to the last page. Those who are already somewhat familiar can safely skip certain sections.

Conventions Used in the Book

Because scripts are often extensive and are hard to read when they're put down on paper (it would be nice if you could support the best optical reading form), I included extra line breaks used to aid readability. Just keep in mind that they have no place in the editor of their development environment.

In general, each program code is set to a non-proportional font. In addition, scripts have line numbers:

```
1   body {
2     color: black;
3   }
```

If you find you need to enter something in the prompt or in a dialog box, that part of the statement is in bold:

$ bower install bootstrap

The first character is the prompt and is not entered. I use the Linux prompt and the bash shell. The commands will work, without any exception, unchanged, even on Windows. The only difference then is the command prompt C:> or something similar is shown at the beginning of the line instead of the $. The instructions are usually related to relative paths or no paths at all, so the actual prompt shouldn't matter despite the fact that you are in your working folder.

Expressions and command lines are sometimes peppered with all types of characters, and in almost all cases, it depends on each character. Often, I'll discuss the use of certain characters in precisely such an expression. Then the "important" characters with line breaks alone and also in this case, line numbers are used to reference the affected symbol in the text exactly (note the : character in line 2):

```
1   a.test {
2     :hover {
3       color: red
4     }
5   }
6
```

The font is non-proportional, so that the characters are countable and opening and closing parentheses are always on their own lines.

Symbols

To facilitate readability, there is a whole range of symbols that are used in the text.

 Tip   This is a tip.

Information   This is extra information.

Warning   This is a warning.

CHAPTER 1

■ ■ ■

Protocols of the Web

This chapter offers a very compact overview of protocols, which you should know if you want to develop web applications actively. The information in this chapter is roughly divided into the following sections:

- The OSI reference model

- The internet protocols family, with TCP/IP and DNS

- The Hypertext Transfer Protocol (HTTP)

- Representational State Transfer (REST)

Standardization with RFCs

If you occupy yourself with protocols or technical procedures of the Internet, you'll always be confronted by RFCs (Request For Comments). The RFCs serve as a public panel for technical and organizational related to the Internet. They were brought to existence in 1969 with ARPANET. RFC 0001 was published on April 7, 1969, during the development of the ARPANET.

RFCs are sequentially numbered can go through different stages. There are no version numbers. If an RFC is comprehensively developed further, a new document with a new number appears. The old is marked as obsolete. If standards are adopted from the RFCs, then these appear in a second document form, which is characterized by an STD. The connection between RFCs and STDs is described in RFC 2500. The standardization process is described in RFC 2026.

As good source of information for RFCs is found at www.rfc-editor.org.[1]

---

[1]http://www.rfc-editor.org

© Jörg Krause 2016
J. Krause, *Introducing Web Development*, DOI 10.1007/978-1-4842-2499-1_1

Here you can comfortably browse the RFC and STD database. If you want to look in greater depth for various information about ICMP or DNS, enter these into the search box, as shown in Figure 1-1.

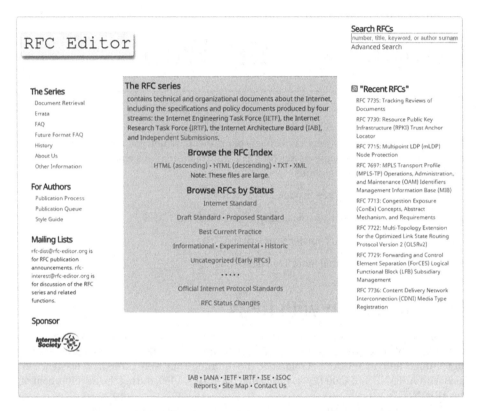

Figure 1-1. *A good source of information is the RFC editor*

The study of RFCS can be quite amusing with the publication date of the first of April of and the status INFORMATIONAL. RFC 2550 is recommended here, in which the year 10.000 problem is discussed.

The OSI Reference Model

For the development and evaluation of communication processes in the IT world, the ISO/OSI reference model is frequently referred to. This model was adopted in 1984 by the ISO (International Organization for Standardization) and describes all the substantial processes during the IP supported data transfer over a layer model. ISO/OSI stands for

Reference Model for Open Systems Interconnection of the International Organization for Standardization.

Table 1-1 shows the seven layers of the ISO/OSI reference model and their meanings.

Table 1-1. *Layers of the ISO/OSI Reference Model*

Nr.	Designation	Task and/or Applications of Examples
7	Application user interface	Program interface
6	Representation	Coding and decoding
5	Meeting communication control	
4	Structure of transport of connections	Data transfer
3	Switching	Addressing and routing of packets
2	Backup, Logical Link Control MAC (Media Access Control)	Control functions, data fragmentation
1	Bit transfer	Physical network transport (cable, radio, etc.)

In the case of a transmission method developed exactly according to this model, one component and/or network protocol works on each level. Between two computer systems, all layers will then go through each case. The actual data exchange takes place finally only over layer 1, for example the network cable. The individual layers within a partner communicate thereby only in each case directly over or under neighbors through protocols and technical components. Thus the higher layers are independent of the process, which takes place further down. Whether layer 1 is technically implemented over a copper or an optical waveguide cable is irrelevant to the protocol layer, which controls the packets to dispatch.

The ISO/OSI reference model is a little theoretical and is in practice rarely consistently converted. The best example of it is at most common network protocols—TCP and IP. The development of these protocols is older than the reference model, so that the so-called Internet protocol family lets itself be only partly illustrated. The motivation for developing its own standardization layer was to simplify and thus decrease the implementation expenditure.

The Internet Protocol Family

The Internet protocol family (Internet Protocol Suite, IPS) can be divided into four layers, which are structured similarly to the reference model. Starting at layer 2, different protocols take over other specific ones in each case. These will be more specifically introduced in the following sections.

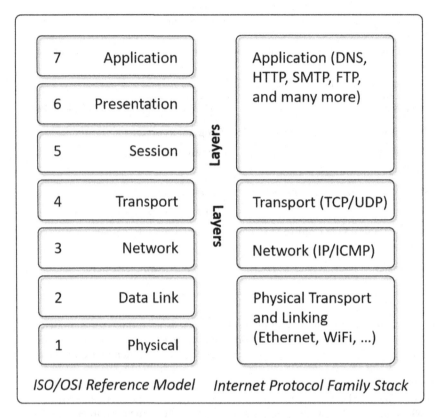

Figure 1-2. Internet protocol family in comparison to the ISO/OSI reference model

Important Protocols of the Internet Protocol Suite

In the following discussion, the most important protocols of the IPS are presented. The sequence corresponds to the IPS 4 layer model (see Figure 1-2).

In Figure 1-2, you can once again see the most important protocols being represented and their classification into the TCP/IP layer model, as well as into the OSI layer model.

The ARP protocols have a special role. Since this is purely technically over the DLCMAC (Ethernet), but doesn't belong to layer 3, it is also sometimes called the 2,5 layer of a protocol.

Address Resolution Protocol (ARP)

This protocol, which works at a very elementary level, allocates the IP addresses of the network adapters of the communication participants. MAC stands for *Media Access Control*. MAC addresses are always worldwide clear, so that a mistake can be excluded from the participants. However, there is a network adapter that permits entering a user-defined MAC address.

The information in the MAC addresses of network computers involved is held in Windows (Server), as with other operating systems in an ARP cache. Thus these do not have to be determined again. You can display the ARP cache with the command prompt ** arp ** (Linux and Windows use the same command) and the option -a.

$ arp -a

If you installed several network adapters in your computer system, you can query the ARP cache for a certain adapter by indicating its IP address:

$ arp -a 192.168.100.6

It's possible to adapt which and how long data is being held in this cache. This is rarely necessary in practice. You can find a more exact description of the syntax ** arp ** and the program with the online help for Windows Server, or on the appropriate main page.

Internet Control Messaging Protocol (ICMP)

This protocol transports the diagnostic, control, and routing packets in the network. It's located on the same layer as IP (Internet Protocol), which is layer 2. ICMP is used for example by the utility program ** ping** in order to inquire information from a host. See Figure 1-3.

```
C:\Users\joerg>ping 8.8.8.8

Pinging 8.8.8.8 with 32 bytes of data:
Reply from 8.8.8.8: bytes=32 time=50ms TTL=49
Reply from 8.8.8.8: bytes=32 time=44ms TTL=49
Reply from 8.8.8.8: bytes=32 time=42ms TTL=49
Reply from 8.8.8.8: bytes=32 time=53ms TTL=49

Ping statistics for 8.8.8.8:
    Packets: Sent = 4, Received = 4, Lost = 0 (0% loss),
Approximate round trip times in milli-seconds:
    Minimum = 42ms, Maximum = 53ms, Average = 47ms
```

Figure 1-3. *Ping on a server (Windows command prompt))*

The server in Figure 1-3 is not a fake address. It concerns the DNA server of Google (google-public-dns-a.google.com).

Internet Protocol (IP)

IP transports the utilizable data in the network. Protocols are characterized by the following features:

- *IP addressing*: Each network can be reached by a clear address, the IP address. Subnet masks create partitions between the subnet work and the concrete host address.

- *No error correction*: The data can be transported over the IP, yet there won't be an error correction.

- *IP fragmentation*: If necessary, packets can be divided over IP into smaller units, especially if the network devices involved are limited.

- *IP broadcast*: Data packets can be sent with IP to a completely determined host, as its IP address is used. This is called *Unicast*. Via an appropriate addressing, several hosts at once can be addressed. This is designated with multicast and used when not meeting-orient data are exchanged, for example, UDP or ICMP data packets. This way, a UDP (multimedia) data stream can be sent to several receivers at the same time.

- *IP routing*: IP is a protocol with the ability of routing. This means that the IP data stream can be led purposefully over an IP router from separate subnetworks to each other.

Since IP belongs to more important protocols in the Web, we should also focus on the exact composition of the head (header), as shown in Figure 1-4.

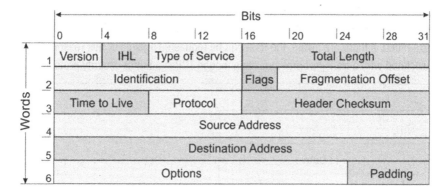

Figure 1-4. *IP header*

- *TOS*

    Apart from the version, the length of the IP head (*IP Header Length*—IHL) and the type of service are indicated. This way devices can prioritize the basic traffic of the data (Type of Service—TOS—is a way of prioritization).

- *Fragmentation*

    The entire package length as well as the fields' identification (it helps with the recognition of fragments), flags (gives information whether the package is fragmented), and FragmentationOffset for building fragmented packages will be indicated.

- *Addresses*

    The most important two fields represent the source (source) as well as the goal (destination) of the address. Here, the IP address is put down byte by byte as a 32-bit (4 bytes) value.

- *Options and Protocol*

    The fields become options (information for the router), time to live (number of switching centers over which a package is conveyed), protocol (which protocol in the IP packages, TCP = 6 or UDP = 17), and a checksum, in order to recognize errors in the head.

ⓘ No Error Correction An error correction is not intended in the IP. This must be made by protocols, which has a layer over it. This is for example the Transmission Control Protocol (TCP). TCP packets "are packed" in addition into IP packages. The TCP packages are then examined. If there are errors, the data can be requested again. For this reason, IP can be associated with a transport protocol, even though TCP is a better security protocol.

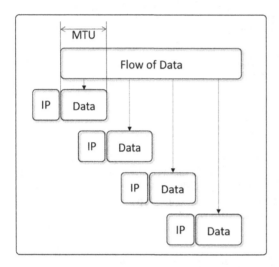

Figure 1-5. *IP fragmentation*

- *MTU*

   The maximum IP package size is named Maximum
   Transmission Unit (MTU). If the package size is smaller
   or equal to the MTU, the package must not be divided but
   fragmented. Fragmented IP packages are characterized as a
   Flag and built up by an appropriate number in the system.
   However, IP fragmentation holds a potential security risk.
   Skillful hackers can, for example, create IP fragments in such
   a way so that the system crashes while it's loading. Therefore,
   IP fragments are rejected by modern firewalls and are usually
   avoided by the procedure Path MTU Discovery. The systems
   involved negotiate the MTU size among themselves.

IPV6 versus V4

The IP protocol may have been specified in version 6 for a long time; however, it takes a while to get started. That may be partially because of the providers and partially because of the manufacturers of the IP equipment. For this reason, IPv4 is still used predominately.

Transmission Control Protocol (TCP)

TCP is a layer above IP and includes an effective mechanism for error correction. Apart from numbering of the data packets, checksums are generated, which check and guarantee the integrity of the data. If an error is recognized, the defective packets are requested; the same happens for packages that weren't loaded at a certain time. That data will be requested again as well.

Since each line has different qualitative features, TCP can adapt the parameters, as to when a package has to be repeated, dynamically. This way, optimal performance is always guaranteed.

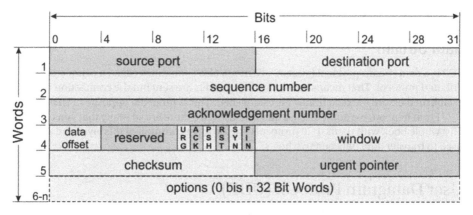

Figure 1-6. *TCP header*

- *Sequence Number*

  The Sequence Number is a sequential number that marks a package in the data stream. That way, packages that arrive in the wrong order can be sorted properly.

- *Acknowledge Number*

  The Acknowledge Number is used to communicate with the receiving station about how many data packages successfully arrived. This way, a new transmission can be released indirectly, if for example it only got approved up to the second-to-last package. The transmitter waits to see whether the packages will be confirmed a bit later than usual (a timeout). If that is not the case, all packages are usually transferred again, starting from the package that wasn't received.

9

- *Window*

  Window is the amount of the data octet (bytes), beginning at
  the data octet indicated by the Acknowledgement field, which
  the transmitter of this TCP is ready to receive.

Port

In addition to the IP source and destination addresses, TCP uses so-called port numbers.
These numbers, combined with the IP addresses, produce a clear connection. Each
service gets a port assigned, which receives detailed connections. Since many unified
services use the same port, a lot of ports are often named after respective services. Here
are a few examples:

- Port 23: Telnet

- Port 80: HTTP-Standard

- Port 21: FTP

Data Stream

TCP is a data stream protocol (stream-oriented), also sometimes called a connection-
oriented protocol. That means that individual packets are sent but the connection is
established before the data transfer is established. This is quite the opposite of UDP.

From here on, we don't discuss other fields, since there are so many that you could
fill a whole book with them. TCP protocols are the most common of this layer and are
used to transfer data between two hosts.

User Datagram Protocol (UDP)

This protocol is related to TC. However, it has different parameters and serves other
purposes. For one, no error connection is implemented. This is not necessary for all
kinds of data transfers. Multimedia streams are, for example, usually transferred with
UDP, since it depends particularly on high performance. If moving pictures miss a few
frames, it won't necessarily be that important. Then that information will transfer, thus
the contents of the film is more important when it arrives at the receiver. Continuous
stagnation during the transmission, because of incorrect or incomplete data, may disturb
your process.

Multimedia and VoIP

UDP is used according to the standard for the inquiry of DNS information. Here protocols
have a high performance advantage at the numerous small packets, which constantly
reach a DNS server. Further applications of this protocol are routing protocols, such as
RIP (Routing Information Protocol), TFTP (Trivial File Transfer Protocol), and SNMP

(Simple Network Management Protocol). In addition, UDP is used with multimedia and other streaming applications like VoIP.

Pay attention, because UDP isn't necessarily the safest protocol due to its missing flow control and error correction. Therefore it is a popular protocol for hackers who use Denial of Service (DoS) attacks again and again. Hosts are flooded with an enormous amount of UD packages, which leads to excessive demand and thus the occasional interruptions in service.

Session Initiation Protocol (SIP)

VoIP (voice over IP) continues to increase in meaning. Even if this book isn't about multimedia and telephony, this protocol enumerates that the most important Internet protocols should not be missing. As the name expresses, this protocol is used for the setting up and communicating sessions for all kinds of uses. You can find further information in the RFC 3261.

The High-Level Language Protocols

High-level language protocols work on layer 7 of the reference model and/or layer 4 of the IPS. They are text-based and usually convey simple commands. For working with web applications, the Hypertext Transfer Protocol (HTTP) is without exception the most important. Aside from that, the File Transfer Protocol (FTP), the Network Transfer Protocol (NNTP), and the Simple Mail Transfer Protocol (SMTP) are all very important as well. Each of these is covered in the following overview.

File Transfer Protocol (FTP)

Besides HTTP, this protocol is the most important for the daily use of the Internet. It serves the data exchange between an FTP server and client, whereby the client can receive access to the file system of the server in a very defined way.

To access an FTP server, all modern operating systems offer different kinds of clients. In addition, there are many FTP clients.

Network News Transfer Protocol (NNTP)

This protocol serves the interaction between so-called news servers and appropriate clients. It is historically seen one of the oldest protocols, and was used far before the introduction of the internet. Protocols work, different than HTTP, statusless, and lead a message to a pointer. For communication with a news server, you must have a registration.

This protocol is now considered outdated. Newsgroups are increasingly replaced by web-based forums, which offer more creative leeway.

Simple Mail Transfer Protocol (SMTP)/Extended SMTP (ESMTP)

SMTP is used by client systems and mail servers for dispatching, as well as sending and passing, e-mails. In the meantime, the ESMTP standard became generally accepted. This is specified in RFC 2821 and offers advanced features for the communication between SMTP client and servers.

Like many other protocols in the Web environment, this protocol is based on ASCII text. All news, which is sent by the client to the server, can be interpreted by both humans and the software.

Hypertext Transfer Protocol (HTTP)

In this section, you learn about HTTP, which plays an outstanding role in web server programming. HTTP serves the communication between web servers. There are three main versions—1.0 (1996, RFC 1945), 1.1 (1999, RFC 2616), and 2.0 (2015, RFC 7540). Most browsers use HTTP 1.1., and some newer browsers (Chrome, Edge) use HTTP 2.0. The version 2.0. is in its introduction phase. In addition, it comes with a set of substandards that are partly implicitly used:

- RFC 7541: Header Compression (2, 2015)

- RFC 7230: Message Syntax and Routing (1.1, 2014)

- RFC 7231: Semantics and Content (1.1, 2014)

- RFC 7232: Conditional Requests (1.1, 2014)

- RFC 7233: Range Requests (1.1, 2014)

- RFC 7234: Caching (1.1, 2014)

- RFC 7235: Authentication (1.1, 2014)

When it comes to HTTP, it's about *connecting* or *statusless protocols*. The server and the client thus never get into special conditions, but terminate the process completely after each command, either with success or with an error message. It is incumbent on the communication partner to react to the message in the appropriate way.

Protocol Construction: Header, Body

HTTP commands are transferred as ASCII text and can consist on several lines. The first line is always the command line. Attached to it is the message header (heading). The heading contains head fields, which describe the command more closely. So it can contain the Content Length head field, for example. If there's any value larger than 0, the data will go into the heading. The data is sent to the message, thus directly together with the command, which might be the Body in that case (message body). HTTP can handle 8-bit values, contrary to other protocols. Binary data, like images and sounds, do not have to be converted. If two blank lines (line changes) follow the HTTP command and the heading lines, the command is considered terminated. Commands with a message body do not have a special ending character. The Content Length head field determines how many bytes make up the contents of the message.

Command Structure

An HTTP command always has the following structure:

```
1   METHOD ID VERSION
```

The command itself is called the METHOD.

ℹ️ Method or Verb? In literature, the HTTP method is sometimes called a *verb*. However, the term verb does not appear in the RFCs and standardization documents. The use of the verb designation comes from classes and data, like `https://technet.microsoft.com/dede/library/dd569062.aspx`, whereby Microsoft methods are called HTTP-Verbs.

Table 1-2 shows the most important HTTP methods at a glance.

Table 1-2. *HTTP Methods*

Method	Meaning
CONNECT	Start the connection to the TLS resources
DELETE	Delete the resource (see REST)
GET	Request the resource
HEAD	Request headers of the resources
LINK	Link two resource requests
OPTIONS	Inquire about the web server's features
POST	Send form data to a server process
PUT	Place resources on the web server (see REST)
TRACE	Send back the command
UNLINK	Delete the link between resources

Consider that the method must be written in capital letters, as shown in Table 1-2. All objects that transfer data are called resources—primarily this includes HTML files and images.

The status code is a three-digit number, and the first number (hundred) shows the allocation to a certain group.

```
1   GET index.html HTTP/1.0
```

This command requests the file index.html.

The HTTP Status Codes

The answer to a command exists in sending the data—if it was requested—and a status code. Optional fields follow the status code and, during the transmission of resources, the data. The status line has the following structure:

```
1   VERSION STATUSCODE STATUSTEXT
```

The status code is a three-digit number, and the first number (hundred) shows the allocation to a certain group.

Table 1-3. *HTTP Reply Code (Selection)*

Group	Code	Name	Meaning
1	100	Continue	Continue further
1	101	Switching Protocols	Protocol change necessary, e.g. HTTP to WebSockets
1	102	Processing	Server works on the request; this is prevented if necessary timeout is longer processing time
2	200	OK	Command successful (after GET/POST)
2	201	Created	Resources are created (after PUT)
2	202	Accepted	Accepts authentication (after GET)
2	204	No Content	No contents or not requested (GET)
3	301	Moved Permanently	Resources at another place
3	302	Found Resource	Temporarily at another place (this is a temporary condition)
3	304	Not Modified	Resources were not changed (steers proxy)
4	400	Bad Request	Syntax error (all commands)
4	401	Unauthorized	No authorization
4	403	Forbidden	Not public range, request inadmissible
4	404	Not Found	Resources not found
5	500	Server Error	Server error, malfunctioning of server software or application
5	503	Service Unavailable	Service not available

You probably know about the 404 error, (not found). You will also become acquainted with the error number 500 (internal server), which is generated if a problem with the code you wrote occurs.

Expiration of HTTP Communication

The fundamental operational sequence of HTTP communication consists of two parts—the request and the answer (response). An HTTP request will look similar to Listing 1-1, whereas Listing 1-2 shows a response.

Listing 1-1. HTTP Request

```
1   GET http://www.joergkrause.de/ HTTP/1.1
2   Accept: text/html, application/xhtml+xml, image/jxr, */*
3   Accept-Language: de-DE,de;q=0.8,en-US;q=0.5,en;q=0.3
4   User-Agent: Mozilla/5.0 (Windows NT 10.0; WOW64; Trident/7.0; LCJB; \
5   rv:11.0) like Gecko
6   Accept-Encoding: gzip, deflate
7   Host: www.joergkrause.de
8   Connection: Keep-Alive
```

Listing 1-2. HTTP Response (Only the Head Fields, Without Data)

```
1    HTTP/1.1 200 OK
2    Date: Sun, 17 Jan 2016 10:59:09 GMT
3    Server: Apache
4    X-Powered-By: PHP/5.5.30
5    Expires: Thu, 19 Nov 1981 08:52:00 GMT
6    Cache-Control: no-store, no-cache, must-revalidate, post-check=0, pr\
7    e-check=0
8    Pragma: no-cache
9    X-Pingback: http://www.joergkrause.de/xmlrpc.php
10   Link: <http://wp.me/P6sMv6-12>; rel=shortlink
11   Set-Cookie: PHPSESSID=4744597c154b01a61e245292b8f1a897; path=/1
12   Keep-Alive: timeout=2, max=200
13   Connection: Keep-Alive
14   Content-Type: text/html; charset=UTF-8
15   Content-Length: 27465
```

Head Fields

Additional fields can be attached to a command or a status line, so-called head fields (sometimes also called headers, because each field stands on its own line):

```
1   Fieldname: Value; Value
```

The heading fields can be divided in three main groups:

- F Question fields (Request Header Fields), which are permitted only in commands.

- A Response fields (Response Header Fields), which are reserved for status news.

- I Information fields (General Header Fields), which serve the transmission of all other news in all directions.

A typical application, which can occur during web programming, is the delivery of a heading field. A special type of file for downloading a file indicates the heading:

```
1    Content-Type: application/pdf; name=aspnet.pdf
```

Contrary to other protocols, the length of a data block is fixed in the content length head field; there are no given separators. Note also that the server does not send an answer to the connection establishment. Only the first arriving command indicates a reaction. The browser must react according to the requirement of an unattainable server in a certain amount of time. A "dead signal" is simply a time interval in which the server should react to the first command.

HTTP 2.0

The current version of HTTP is 2.0 (called HTTP/2 in the header), which was published as RFC 7540 on the May 15th, 2015.

The standard is today specified in the RFCs 7540 and 7541. Google has considerably improved its development (*SPDY*, which is pronounced like "speedy'). Microsoft (HTTP Speed + Mobility) also has its own case in each proposal. A first draft, which was to a large extent against SPDY, was published in November 2012 and was adapted in several steps.

With HTTP/2, the transmission is accelerated and optimized. The new standard is completely downward compatible with HTTP/1.1.

Important new features include:

- Summarizing several requests

- Better compression possibilities

- Binary transmissions of coded contents

- Server-initiated data transfer (push procedures)

An acceleration results mainly from the new possibility of summarizing (multiplex) several requests, in order to be able to complete them over a connection. The data compression now also includes head data. Instead of the Gzip or Deflated used thus far, you can use a new special algorithm called HPACK.

Contents can be coded in binary. In order to not have to wait for subsequent client requirements, the data transfer can be partly initiated by the server (push procedures).

The originally planned option that HTTP/2 use TLS (Transport Layer Security, called SSL back then and useful for encoding) according to the standard, was not converted. However, Google and Mozilla announced for their browsers that HTTP/2 will not have any support without encoding (see Application Layer Protocol Negotiation). Due to market power, one must assume therefore that all HTTP/2 servers will compellingly offer TLS.

The most popular browsers now support HTTP/2. This includes Google Chrome (also iOS and Android) starting at version 41, Mozilla Firefox starting at version 36, Internet Explorer 11 under Windows 10, Opera starting at version 28 (also Opera Mobile starting from version 24), and Safari starting at version 8.

Supplemental Standards

HTTP is flanked by other standards, which either add to it or use it as a supplement.

WebSockets

The WebSocket protocol is a TCP-based network protocol, and it has been created in order to achieve a bidirectional connection between a web application and a WebSocket server and/or a web sever that supports WebSockets. The additional data may fall away because of the HTTP head fields in association with WebSockets.

The request is initiated with a special head field from HTTP:

```
1   GET /chat HTTP/1.1
2   Host: server.example.com
3   Upgrade: websocket
4   Connection: Upgrade
5   Sec-WebSocket-Key: dJhoIeNrbgBKZrBabu5sZe==
6   Origin: http://example.com
7   Sec-WebSocket-Protocol: chat, superchat
8   Sec-WebSocket-Version: 13
```

The answer should then contain the status code 101:

```
1   HTTP/1.1 101 Switching Protocols
2   Upgrade: websocket
3   Connection: Upgrade
4   Sec-WebSocket-Accept: sjpoLeBrTgai9sYazGheRe+KxOo=
5   Sec-WebSocket-Protocol: chat
```

Due to the HTTP status code 101 and the following two lines, the server explains that it agrees with the exchange of protocols.

If you try to see it in a technical way, WebSocket client, just like with HTTP, starts a request. The difference is that, after the transmission of data, the connection establishment and the underlying TCP connection remain and transmissions in both directions are possible.

WebDAV

WebDAV (Web-based Distributed Authoring and Versioning) is an open standard for the supply of files on the internet. Users can access its data transparently, thus they can read and write to it.

WebDAV is an extension of the protocol HTTP/1.1, but it waives certain restrictions of HTTP. With WebDAV files, whole listings can be transferred. Besides that, the version control is specified.

Since granting write access to web servers is rather risky, WebDAV hasn't been very popular. It is useful, if at all, for publishing applications in a local development environment. Some web hosts and providers offer it as efficient alternative to FTP.

REST

REST stands for *Representational State Transfer* and marks an architectural style (or a "programming paradigm for distributed systems"; see https://de.wikipedia.org/wiki/Representationa State_Transfer). It summarizes already frequently used techniques and protocols for data transfer. This covers:

- URI for addressing resources

- HTTP for transmitting commands

- MIME for coding resources

- JSON and XML for formatting

 Web Service   REST is a special form of web service. One therefore speaks of a *REST service*.

Features

The technical features of a REST service are:

- Addressability

- Representation variable

- Conditionlessness

- Scalability

- General acceptance

- Expandability

Addressability

Each REST service has a clear address, called the *Uniform Resource Locator* (URL). REST also uses a *Uniform Resource Identifier* (URI) in order to designate individual resources.

Representation Variable

The address-accessible services can have different representational forms (representations). A REST server can supply HTML, JSON, or XML, for example. This can contain data or descriptions.

Conditionlessness

Each REST message contains all the information necessary for the server and/or the client in understand the message. Neither the server nor the application store status information between the news. It's a stateless protocol. Each request contains all the information about the application's condition, which is needed by the server.

Scalability

The conditionlessness favors the scalability of a service. Since each request leads to a defined reaction and no condition on a certain machine has to be there, load divider requests can be distributed on several machines. Without that, this changes the server site processing.

Generally Accepted

HTTP prescribes that GET must be "safe". This means that this method has only information and no side effects. The methods GET, HEAD, PUT, and DELETE must be idempotent, which means that repeated sending of the same requirement does not change it.

Expandable

Extensibility means that extensions of resource base, additional functions, more data, other representations, or other scaling measures taking place later won't affect the existing clients.

REST Example

One characteristic of REST is the description of resources. The elements be included or left off. If relationships exist between the data, then this is to be recognized in the answer. One simple inquiry uses the GET command (see also section about HTTP later in this chapter).

```
1   GET /book/2605
```

```
1   HTTP/1.1 200 OK Content-Type: text/xml
2   <?xml version="1.0"?>
3   <book xmlns:xlink="http://www.w3.org/1999/xlink">
4       <cat xlink:href="http://shop.texxtoor.de/cat/122">122</cat>
5       <author xlink:href="http://shop.texxtoor.de/author/1">1</author>
6       <author xlink:href="http://shop.texxtoor.de/author/2">2</author>
7       <title>Pug</title>
8       <desc>The Template-Engine Pug</desc>
9       <price>2,99</price>
10      <type>Paperback</type>
11  </book>
```

Here, URI refers to some elements of dependent resources. The client can use this to provide a part of the user interface dynamically.

URI

URI stands for *Uniform Resource Identifier* and is the procedure for designing the addresses. In connection with REST, the term *RESTful* means that the correct implementation of REST is used. That means not only that HTTP is used, but also that the routes, which call the data and release actions, obey certain criteria.

URI is often confused with URL (Uniform Resource Locater). URL is a special form of URI. URLs serve the addressing of web pages in the browser. URIs can address web pages and other things. URLs attach data parameters, which are separated by ?. This is called the *querystring*. Here are some typical applications:

- /admin/updatebook.aspx?book=2605

- /bookview.html?book=2605

- /bookreviews.py?book=2605

The book=2605 part is the querystring. This is **not** RESTful. REST requires that the data division be part of the URL. *Routes*—addressing patterns on the basis of the URI—have defined sections, to which meaning is assigned. This assignment is arbitrary (point of developing), but frequently rungs according to a simple principle:

```
/resource/id
```

Or a somewhat more complex principle:

`/resource/id/action`

RESTful examples look as follows:

- `/admin/book/2605`
- `/book/2605`
- `/book/2605/view`

Certainly here are still many options present. Therefore, a few rules:

- *Short*: Shorter URIs are better
- *Tree structure*: The tree structure of the object/data graph should represent the URI.
- *Readable*: Plain language helps
- *Predictable*: The reaction of the server makes sense based on URI name.
- **Nouns**: URIs address *something*, therefore the word is not a thing, an action. If an action is used, it attaches itself from behind.
- **Querystring** I: You can use them, but only exactly as query (inquiries/searches), for example:

  `/books/search?filter=title&value=JADE`

- **Querystring II**: Don't use if parameters are needed, for example:

  `/books/select/quarter=2;year=2016`

- *Deterministic*: The same resources always show the same URI.
- *Stateless*: No condition on the server has influence.
- *Canonical*: If two URIs lead to the same resource, the alternative in the answer must be designated.

Less important, but still important for good style, are these guidelines:

- Only use lowercase: CamelCase and the like are rather disturbing in this setting.
- Use hyphens instead of underlines: *book-review* is better than *book_review* for search engines.
- Use plural, if applicable (*books*, if it concerns several).

- If a call for collections takes place, this should be visible: /books/
  book/3. Then, however, the call must be technically possible, such
  as /books and supply all books. However, if the collection cannot
  be supplied, /book/3 is enough.

- No blanks: Sooner or later you'll see only %20 fragments (indicates
  a blank coded for an URL)

HTTP

REST uses specific HTTP methods in order to release actions on the server. REST uses
these HTTP methods:

- GET: Call up resources

- POST: Change or release an action

- PUT: Produce s resource

- DELETE: Delete resources

- PATCH: Change a part of a resource

- HEAD: Request meta-data

- OPTIONS: Show permitted actions on resources

It is not compellingly necessary to compare this to SQL; a simple mapping, however,
can represent REST well, as shown in Table 1-4.

Table 1-4. Mapping REST to SQL

HTTP (REST)	SQL
GET	SELECT
POST	INSERT
PUT	UPDATE
DELETE	DELETE

In HTTP, this looks as follows (. . . stands for typical head fields):

```
1   POST /book/2605
2   ...
3   name=New Article
```

Here, the URI is a relative path to resources. basket marks the route to a controller,
which worries about the car. The route expects an ID, which is 2605 here. Thus an
element has the primary key 2605 in the cart. This element has a feature called name to
which the new text "new article name" is assigned.

By means of PUT resources are produced as follows:

```
1   PUT /book
2
3   <book>
4     <title>Pug</title>
5     <desc>
6       The Template-Engine Pug
7     </desc>
8     <price>2,99</price>
9     <type>Paperback</type>
10  </book>
```

Since one of the characteristics of REST is self description, PUT returns a link to new resources:

```
1   HTTP/1.1 201 OK
2   Content-Type: text/xml;
3   Content-Length: 34
4
5   http://shop.texxtoor.de/book/2605
```

Deleting resources takes place similarly:

```
1   DELETE /book/2605
```

MIME

MIME stands for *Multipurpose Internet Mail Extensions* and was originally developed to embed documents in e-mails. A describing header is used in order to show the original format. The client can then re-create it. It's divided into two parts and includes the header, which is the typical "content type":

```
group/detail
```

For an image, it looks as follows:

```
Content-Type: image/jpeg
```

A specification, which is needed here and goes beyond REST, can be found at https://de.wikipedia.org/wiki/Multipurpose_-Internet_Mail_Extensions.

For REST, the following is used:

- text/xml
- application/json

JSON

For communication between a client and a server, JSON is used. JSON (JavaScript Object Notation) is a compact format in readable text form for the purpose of data exchange between applications. Although the name points to an exclusive use in JavaScript, JSON is an independent format, and it can be used in any programming language.

The biggest difference between JSON and XML is the somewhat more compact coding of data structures where, contrary to XML, less administrative data is produced. In addition JSON can be converted into JavaScript or directly into a JavaScript object. However, XML is more versatile than JSON and applicable, which is not a markup language, but a data exchange format. XML enjoys a bigger audience. Both formats are not necessary to represent large binary data.

JSON recognizes objects, arrays, character strings, numbers, Boolean values, and zero. Data can be interlocked at will, for example, an array of objects is possible. JSON uses UTF-8 as its indication coding.

The JSON Format Definition

A JSON object is surrounded by curly braces { }. It can contain an unordered list of characters, divided by commas.

A characteristic JSON object consists of a key and a value, separated by a colon. The key is a character string. The value is an object, an array, a character, a string, a number, or one of the expressions true, false, or zero. An array begins and ends with square brackets [ ]. It can contain a regulatory list of values, divided by commas.

A character string begins and ends with quotation marks ("). It can contain Unicode characters and escape sequences. A Boolean value is represented by the expressions true or false without quotation marks. A number is in the range of 0-9 and can include a minus sign – by the way of introduction and a decimal point, if interrupted. The number can be supplemented by the information of an exponent e or E, which can have a sign such as + or -. It also recognizes empty space characters arbitrarily.

Listing 1-3. Example of a JSON Block

```
 1   {
 2       "CreditCard"      : "Visa",
 3       "Number"          : "1234-5678-9012-3456",
 4       "Owner"           :
 5       {
 6         "LastName"      : "Krause",
 7         "Firstname"     : "Jörg",
 8         "Gender"        : "\"male\"",
 9         "Preferences"   : [
10           "Golf",
11           "Reading",
12           "Badminton"
13         ],
14         "Age"           : null
15       },
```

```
16      "Limit"       : 10000,
17      "Currency"    : "EURO"
18  }
```

If you'd like to read more about JSON, the following sources might be interesting:

- json.org offers an introduction to the official JSON site.

- The RFC 4627 defines a further type of MIME with application/json.

The ATOM Format

ATOM stands for the *Atom Syndication Format*, an platform-independent format used to change feeds. It has the same purpose as the well-known RSS, the Really Simple Syndication. ATOM is considered a designated successor of RSS 2.0. ATOM is defined for different purposes, whereby the ASF (ATOM Syndication Format) is referred here. Apart from the pure feed distribution, ATOM can be used for newsletters and similar purposes. ATOM was published in RFC 4278. The type of MIME is application/atom+xml. Listing 1-4 shows a typical ATOM block.

Listing 1-4. Typical ATOM Block

```
1   <?xml version="1.0" encoding="utf-8"?>
2   <feed xmlns="http://www.w3.org/2005/Atom">
3     434759_1_En
4       <name>Jörg Krause</name>
5     </author>
6     <id>urn:uuid:60a76c80-9926-9905-1964-0003939e0af6</id>
7
8     <entry>
9       <title>Neues aus der Web-Welt</title>
10      <link href="http://hanser.de/2010/08/08/atom-wcf"/>
11      <id>urn:uuid:1225c695-cfb8-4ebb-aaaa-01723243189a</id>
12      <updated>2016-12-08T12:50:07Z</updated>
13      <summary>Alles über Web</summary>
14      <content>Hier steht der gesamte Text</content>
15    </entry>
16  </feed>
```

Atom in Web Sites   In web applications, use ATOM only if your clients demand it explicitly. The employment of JSON is clearly simpler and faster.

CHAPTER 2

Dynamic Web Sites

This chapter is about quickly and clearly covering the execution when calling up dynamic web pages. Some aspects of optimization are also discussed. It is helpful to never forget about optimization when you're creating your web site.

How Dynamic Web Sites Are Created

Dynamic web pages are known as pages that are created as soon as a call is sent to the server. So data can be built interactively into the sites. They are particularly helpful when you need to react to user inputs. Forms can be evaluated immediately and the content of the next page can be shown. The application possibilities are nearly unlimited. Whether and to which extent databases are used depends on the goal. Dynamic web pages actually do not need a database. You should not feel obligated to solve every problem with the help of a database when you're a beginner, while professionals may recommend that.

This book shows many examples that obtain impressing effects with the simplest means—completely without a database. The emergence of a dynamic web site is described with the help of an illustration. You should understand this execution well, because all other, more complex, procedures in programming depend on it.

If the user types an address in the browser, a complex procedure happens:

1. The browser looks for a name server in order to determine the IP address to the URL.

2. The name sever may necessarily consult with further servers, in order to procure the IP address.

3. The browser receives an IP address of the sever. If the HTTP protocol is used, the port address is also fixed (Port 80). The IP address and port form a so-called *socket*.

4. The browser receives an IP address from the provider and forms a port for the connection. Thus, a socket is available. Between both terminals, IP traffic can now take place.

5. The browser sends the requirement via the connection to the site. This happens with the HTTP protocol. The appropriate method reads GET, the procedure is called request or requirement.

© Jörg Krause 2016
J. Krause, *Introducing Web Development*, DOI 10.1007/978-1-4842-2499-1_2

6. The server receives the requirement and looks for the file. If it's found, it will be delivered. This procedure is called response and in this book, it's also called answer. If the file is not found, the server produces an error. For missing files, HTTP defines the error number 404.

7. The browser receives data or an error message and shows these.

First the user requests a program using his browser. The entire procedure is client-steered in the long run. On this web server the request is accepted and HTML code or static contents will be created. Thus the procedure is terminated. Both sides "forget" everything that happened during this procedure. With the requirement of the next object, the entire operational sequence is repeated. The procedures of the name resolution and address procurement happen completely transparent and are hardly noticed when programming. The actual assembly of the sites is the interesting part. This happened in the representation of the signal element sequence in Step 6. We will examine this step in more detail.

For all problems, various programming environments supply interesting and helpful solutions. Programming is therefore comparatively simple. However, that changes nothing in the principle of the underlying technology. Without the ping-pong play between browsers and web servers, nothing would function. Sometimes it's not always visible that this process actually happens, but it is nevertheless without exception implemented. Clearly it should be remembered that, if the web site request is sent to the browser, only HTML code is produced.

Optimization

During the optimization, there are many aspects to consider:

- Development environment: Without the correct tools it won't work!

- Server-page optimization: Requests, range, and payload

- Client-page optimization: DOOM and JavaScript

Tools

Try to understand how the Web functions. In addition you have to know other things aside from the already covered protocols, such as performance, range, and the number of HTTP requests, since the behavior of HTML and JavaScript usually differentiate when rendering the CSS effects in the browser. Various tools help make the procedures visible and this helps substantially to understand them.

You should have the following tools:

- Fiddler:

    - From Telerik, for Windows (http://www.telerik.com/fiddler)

    - Fiddler on Mono (http://fiddler.wikidot.com/mono) for Linux

- F12—Tools in IE, Chrome, Firefox, Edge, etc. :

    - Profiler

    - Network Analytics

    - CSS-Debugger

    - HTML-Tree

    - JavaScript Debugger

- Also available online:

    - Pingdom[1]

    - Browserstack[2]

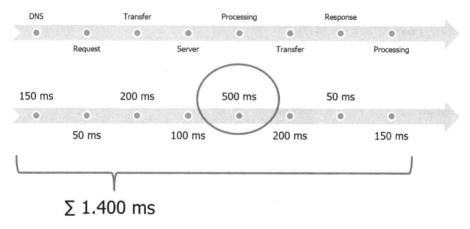

Figure 2-1. *Execution of communication on a timeline*

Fiddler is a web debugger and a protocol proxy. Thus you can see and evaluate the traffic between the client and server. In terms of temporal operational sequence, the requests really happen only partly in parallel. Some inquiries are only released when the browser starts processing the site.

---

[1]http://tools.pingdom.com/fpt
[2]http://www.browserstack.com

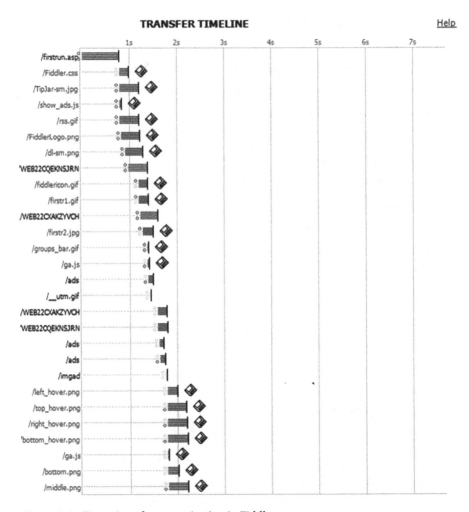

Figure 2-2. *Execution of communication in Fiddler*

These effects can be considered within the structure of the site. The less dependence there is, the better the range that's available.

Server Page Optimization

The server-page optimization stage involves the following topics:

- Pipeline optimization
- Process configuration
- CDN
- Bundling
- Sprites

Pipeline Optimization

At the core, it concerns unloading (to deactivate) unnecessary modules. Web servers come with a whole set of modules, which fulfill all possible tasks. This begins with authentication and ends with simple logging. It's in the nature of these modules that they treat each request. Small delays can have drastic effects.

For ASP.NET and IIS, it looks like Figure 2-3, which shows first the active standard modules.

```
<httpModules>
    <add name="OutputCache" type="System.Web.Caching.OutputCacheModule" />
    <add name="Session" type="System.Web.SessionState.SessionStateModule" />
    <add name="WindowsAuthentication" type="System.Web.Security.WindowsAuthenticationModule" ,
    <add name="FormsAuthentication" type="System.Web.Security.FormsAuthenticationModule" />
    <add name="PassportAuthentication" type="System.Web.Security.PassportAuthenticationModule'
    <add name="RoleManager" type="System.Web.Security.RoleManagerModule" />
    <add name="UrlAuthorization" type="System.Web.Security.UrlAuthorizationModule" />
    <add name="FileAuthorization" type="System.Web.Security.FileAuthorizationModule" />
    <add name="AnonymousIdentification" type="System.Web.Security.AnonymousIdentificationModu:
    <add name="Profile" type="System.Web.Profile.ProfileModule" />
    <add name="ErrorHandlerModule" type="System.Web.Mobile.ErrorHandlerModule, System.Web.Mob:
    <add name="ServiceModel" type="System.ServiceModel.Activation.HttpModule, System.ServiceM
    <add name="UrlRoutingModule-4.0" type="System.Web.Routing.UrlRoutingModule" />
```

Figure 2-3. *Modules with IIS: not optimized*

Possibly only some of it is really needed, as shown in Figure 2-4.

```
<httpModules>
    <!-- Remove unnecessary Http Modules for faster pi|
    <remove name="Session" />
    <remove name="WindowsAuthentication" />
    <remove name="PassportAuthentication" />
    <remove name="AnonymousIdentification" />
    <remove name="UrlAuthorization" />
    <remove name="FileAuthorization" />
```

Figure 2-4. *Modules in IIS: optimized*

If you work with Apache on Linux, use the command a2dismod:

```
$ sudo a2dismod autoindex
```

Typical modules, which are not always needed, are the following:

- PHP
- SSL
- Rewrite
- Perl
- Python
- Rack/Ruby/Passenger

Process Configuration

The goal here is the optimal use of resources. In addition you adapt the process configuration to the concrete hardware conditions. For a Windows server, IIS covers the following steps:

- **maxWorkerThreads**

  20 per core (4 cores == 80 threads). More is possible, if there is CPU-intensive work (e.g., much async, service calls), then values to 100 are possible.

- **maxIOThreads**

  20 per core. For file operations, database access, web service calls, internal requests etc. with fast hardware, SSD etc., values up to 100 are possible for a 10Gbit net.

- **minWorkerThreads, minIOThreads**

  Standard 1. Steers the beginning of the request queue. At least the value must be free, so that it will not be queued.

- **memoryLimit**

  Portion (%) of the system memory that the worker process may occupy. If the application is alone, the value may be high, e.g., 80. With many lags or other applications, COM will reduce the value.

Settings of the process configuration take place in machine.config, as shown in Figure 2-5.

```
<system.web>
    <processModel autoConfig="true"/>
```

Figure 2-5. *Settings of process configuration*

In Apache, you configure comparable values as follows:

```
1    <IfModule mpm_worker_module>
2    ServerLimit              40
3    StartServers              2
4    MaxClients             1000
5    MinSpareThreads          25
6    MaxSpareThreads          75
7    ThreadsPerChild          25
8    MaxRequestsPerChild       0
9    </IfModule>
```

CDN (Content Delivery Network)

A Content Delivery Network (sometimes called a Content Distribution Network) is regionally distributed and makes it possible to deliver content, such as scripts, pictures, and videos, over the Internet. The goal of a CDN is quicker answers to requests and less latency. For general files, like jQuery, Knockout, etc. Microsoft, Google etc. will be there for you. For your own resources, you are liable to pay the costs for services such as CacheFly (simple, upload/distribute) and EdgeCast (complex, DNS catching).

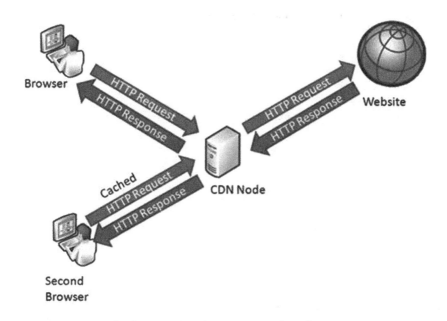

Figure 2-6. *Principle of a Content Delivery Network (CDN)*

Minify and Bundling

Bundling and minifying are two techniques that can improve load time. This essentially happens by summarizing resources (bundling) and avoiding requests. Due to the overhead of HTTP protocols, it requires the distribution of many small files, while it has more bandwidth than a large file.

The creation of sprites is not really manually controllable. Therefore, a variety of tools for all platforms and operating systems is provided. Ideally you furnish these tools as part of the production procedure. How it looks depends on the development system.

Sprites

An individual diagram file, which contains several symbols and picture components, is called a *sprite* or a *CSS sprite*. These summarized diagrams function as picture suppliers and serve to minimize the load time of the web pages. The individual elements of this total diagram faded out of place with the background-image and background-position CSS characteristics.

Due to the overhead of HTTP protocols, the distribution of many small pictures requires more range, as the distribution of a larger picture.

Here is an example of CSS that works with sprites:

```
1   .flags-canada, .flags-mexico, .flags-usa {
2       background-image: url('../images/flags.png');
3       background-repeat: no-repeat;
4   }
5
6   .flags-canada {
7       height: 128px;
8       background-position: -5px -5px;
9   }
10
11  .flags-usa {
12      height: 135px;
13      background-position: -5px -143px;
14  }
15
16  .flags-mexico {
17      height: 147px;
18      background-position: -5px -288px;
19  }
```

The creation of sprites is not really controllable. Therefore, a variety of tools for all platforms and operating systems is provided. You can do this under a node or on a system, that has installed a node. Take Sprity as an example. This is how you install it:

```
$ npm install sprity -g
```

Then you combine all the pictures of a folder into sprites:

```
$ sprity ./outputfolder/ ./inputfolder/*.png
```

 You can find more examples at `https://css-tricks.com/css-sprites`.

General and Banal

Generally, you should be sure not to use these certain techniques:

- Try to avoid redirects
- Try to avoid frames/iframes
- Try to avoid DNS lookups (absolute paths)

Spreading assets on various hosts is called *off-loading* and looks like this:

- `www.greatsite.com`
- `images.greatsite.com`
- `scripts.greatsite.com`

Essentially, browsers only send a certain number of requests per host (between 6 and 13) and if you have three hosts, this triples the available range.

With static assets you should avoid cookies and headers, if possible. Absolutely use Gzip/Deflate for compression. It should be available on practically all systems. Then configure the server in such a way that it uses Gzip. ETag (entity brand) is not needed—you can remove this head field if you want to.

Client-Site Optimization

Here is only a short overview of the possibilities. These are simply suggestions, and you can find many more examples on the Internet.

Handling Pictures

If modern browsers are available, use inline pictures. Particularly for dynamic pictures, for rare or frequently changing ones, this method is favorable.

```
1    <img src="data:image/gif;base64, R0lGODlh...
2            ....        and so on .... ">
```

The coding of Base64 is suitable, such as `http://webcodertools.com/imagetobase64converter`.

You should never scale pictures, but always compute them before (on the server) and compress them before delivering.

Use font libraries, so-called *symbol fonts,* if possible. Font-based symbols are more streamlined, whereas individual pictures and symbols have more stringent requirements. All symbols are loaded as fonts, thus they exist in a file. However, symbols are more like letters. Their size can change, but they can only accept one color. Fonts are mostly fine, if you don't mind the 3D effect ones. For fast, modern web pages, Glyphs is far more established.

Some examples:

- Font Awesome[3]: 479 symbols

- Octicons, the GitHub Icons[4]: 160 symbols

- Elegant Icon Font[5]: 350 symbols

- Typicons[6]: 336 symbols

- Meteocons[7]: 40 Weather symbols

- Open Iconic[8]: 223 symbols that can't be reduced to eight pixels

This is certainly only a small selection. Be sure to search around to find options that meet your exact needs.

---

[3]http://fortawesome.github.io/Font-Awesome/
[4]https://octicons.github.com/
[5]http://www.elegantthemes.com/blog/resources/elegant-icon-font
[6]http://typicons.com
[7]http://www.alessioatzeni.com/meteocons
[8]https://useiconic.com/open

Figure 2-7. *The free symbol font octicons*

If you use JPG files, try to remove any junk data. This is the meta-information that adds cameras, partly in programs such as Photoshop. Kilobytes of information are wasted that way, such as for date, camera data, etc.

Generally pay attention to the suitable image format.

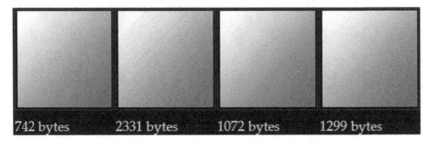

Figure 2-8. *Image size with pictures and color processes*

Handling the DOM

The JavaScript language is extremely fast. What's problematic is accessing elements in the object tree of the site (document object model, DOM). To illustrate this, look at this jQuery example:

```
1  $('#dialog-window')
2    .width(600)
3    .height(400)
4    .css('position': 'absolute')
5    .css('top', '200px')
6    .css('left', '200px');
```

An element gets addressed as #dialog-window and is accessed six times in a row. This is very unfortunate. It's better to do it the following way, which changes all values with one access:

```
1  $('#dialog-window').css({
2    width: '600px',
3    height: '400px',
4    position: 'absolute',
5    top: '200px',
6    left: '200px' });
```

Here a batch is provided when rendering. Provide dynamic DOM blocks separately and insert the entire tree in one step. This leads to the screen refreshing on many indication procedures. You should know that the browser draws the surface each time the DOM is changed. Sequences with many small changes require a substantial amount of computing power. Even if this is available, it means nevertheless a lot of battery service life will be used if you're using a mobile device.

CHAPTER 3

■ ■ ■

HTML: Hypertext Markup Language

The basis of every web site is the specification language it uses, HTML (HyperText Markup Language). It structures the sites, and the current version HTML5 can access hierarchical object models of the site, which are accessed via JavaScript. CSS (Cascading Style Sheets) organize the graphic contents of the site.

Both languages are very old and meet today's requirements insufficiently. HTML5 became therefore a bundle of different standards, which supplements all kinds of functions. An overview is described in this chapter. In addition, different template systems were established, and they attempt to address the disadvantages of HTML. AngularJS tries to work after the intentions of its developers and is something like a dynamic extension, although it would be different if it had been invented together with HTML.

Even CSS isn't new. Here, complex style systems make high demands, whereupon there are two answers. On the one hand, preprocessors like LESS and SASS were developed, which define dynamic CSS and are prepared for the modern-day browser.

Basics of HTML

This section is about the basics of HTML, including a very short historical overview.

The History of HTML

The HTML standard is a cooperation between the W3C (World Wide Web Consortium) and the WHATWG (Web Hypertext Application Technology Working Group). The principles of the working groups are:

- The standard is HTML + CSS + DOM + JavaScript

- No plugins (no Java, no Flash, no Silverlight, nothing!)

- More markup, don't be obtrusive, less direct scripting

- Device-independence

© Jörg Krause 2016
J. Krause, *Introducing Web Development*, DOI 10.1007/978-1-4842-2499-1_3

Your own implementations should follow these principles!

Figure 3-1. *The official HTML5 logo*

Table 3-1. *The History of the HTML Versions*

Version	Year
HTML	1991
HTML+	1993
HTML2	1995
HTML3.2	1997
HTML4.01	1999
XHTML1.1	2001
WHATWG	2004
WHATWG and W3C Cooperation	2006
HTML5	2012
XHTML5	2013
HTML5.2	2015 - 2016

XML Basics for HTML

Even though the topic of this chapter is HTML, you should know the basic structure of an XML document. Both standards use the same ideology and are so-called *markup languages*. This term is the reason behind ML. Contrary to programming languages, markup languages serve to describe contents. Here, only the most necessary characteristics are discussed.

40

Markup

All tag groups whose structure is defined in XML is called markup:

- Start tags: `<startTag>`

- End tags: `</endTag>`

- Empty elements: `<EmptyElement />`

- Entity references: `&amp;`

- Character references: `&x0f;`

- Comments: `<!-- Comment -->`

- CDATA range limiter: `<![CDATA[ no XML ]]>`

- Document type declarations: `<!DOCTYPE HTML PUBLIC "-//W3C//DTD HTML 4.01 Transitional//EN" "http://www.w3.org/TR/html4/loose.dtd"`

- Instructions for processing: `<? include ("datei.php") ?>`

- The XML declaration: `<?xml version="1.0"?>`

- Text declaration: `<?xml encoding="utf-8" ?>`

Everything else is text. Three special characters steer the markup:

- `&gt;` stands for <

- `&lt;` stands for >

- `&amp;` stands for &

For attribute values and quotes, two entities are added:

- `&quot;` stands for "

- `&apos;` stands for '

CDATA ranges represent a special feature. In these, the usual rules are repealed and special indications must not be coded:

```
<![CDATA[ here & here is "not" <XML> ]]>
```

Structure and Features of an XML Document

The XML document structure follows firm rules. These rules enable an automated processing system in a comprehensive to take place. On the other hand, the employment should be as universal as possible, as the name "eXtensible Markup Language" suggests.

Shapeliness

The rules permit the examination of the shapeliness of documents by the processing program without knowledge of the grammar of the language. The term shapeliness, which means "well formed," is a basic characteristic of markup languages. A document is considered shapely if the following features apply:

- All tags are syntactically correct. All beginning tags have an end tag, whereby upper- and lowercase are to be considered (`<tag></Tag>` is inadmissible). Each opening tag must have a closing tag (`<tag></tag>`). Alternatively, one tag can be closed directly (`<tag/>`).

- All attributes are syntactically correct. Parameters of the attributes must always be placed in quotation marks (`<tag attr= "param">`). In addition, shortened attributes, those without parameters, are not permitted. The HTML tag `<hr noshade>` would look in XHTML (the corresponding HTML in XML) as follows: `<hr noshade= "noshade"/>`.

- Correct nesting is necessary. Tags must be correctly interlocked. The following code is wrong: `<b><i></b></i>`. Instead, it has to be written as follows: `<b><i></i></b>`.

Validation

In a second processing step, the grammar must be naturally checked. It concerns their relation permitted tags, and the possibly applicable attributes. This step is called *validation*. A document must be recognizable as valid before processing. A regulation must naturally exist for validation, from which the parser can derive the validity, and there are several procedures.

Processing

During the processing of the data, there are different strategies. One of them illustrates the document as an object model in a hierarchy. Wrongly interlocked tags do not permit the representation as a hierarchy. A hierarchy is most simply represented as a tree.

The Term "Markup"

HTML, XML, and XHTML are all markup languages, and they are based on SGML. SGML stands for Standard Generalized Markup Language and was developed in 1986. HTML and XML descend directly from SGML. XML is more restrictive than SGML and serves as a basis for XHTML. XHTML is identical to HTML, except the spellings are based on XML (see Figure 3-2).

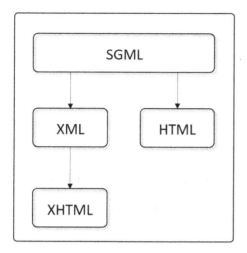

Figure 3-2. *Development of basic standards*

The empty elements are a feature, but not a necessity.

Empty Elements

Empty elements do not have contents. They produce an edition, have a standard behavior, and are shapeable in some cases.

The most well-known empty elements are:

```
1    <br>
2    <hr>
3    <img>
4    <input>
5    <link>
6    <meta>
```

The following empty elements are rarely used in HTML:

```
1    <area>
2    <base>
3    <col>
4    <command>
5    <embed>
6    <keygen>
7    <param>
8    <source>
9    <track>
10   <wbr>
```

So it is not permitted to be written as
</br>. Alternatively to the classical HTML, –
 can be always used with the XHTML variants of the immediate closing tag: <br/>. So far, so good. But why is this possible? The reason is to look back long ago, in SGML.

43

A so-called null end tag (NET) was permitted in SGML. It was an abbreviation, in order to avoid the closing tag. With NET, you can write the following:

```
<quote/Quoted text/
```

Without NET, it would look as follows:

```
<quote>Quoted text</quote>
```

The short version for elements without contents is called `<quote//` (`SHORTTAG NETENABL IMMEDNET`), which corresponds to `<quote></quote>`.

HTML attempted to take over this feature and close elements like XML correctly. That is because the `<br/` would be wrong in this case, and a `<br/>` as `<br>>` would be just as wrong. The "correct" slash is here the error. With the implementation the browser developers considered this and did not adopt the SGML typical spelling. In this case, HTML leans more strongly against XML. In HTML5 it was still theoretically permitted and the SGML spelling was explicitly forbidden.

XML (and thus XHTML) serves to avoid the problems of this syntax completely. In order to make empty elements possible, a special spelling is used: `<b/>`. The slash in the end returned, and it is now correctly placed between the `<` and `>` delimiters.

Validity

The validity of HTML results from the correct construction of tags. An element is considered a tag, and it obeys certain rules:

- It must begin with a `<` indication.

- It must be followed directly by the name of the element (`<name>`).

- It follows attributes, which are always limited by blanks (this is optional).

- If the element is empty, it will be closed with `/>`, otherwise with `>`.

ℹ️ Especially in HTML5, the closing `/>` tag construct is optional. The HTML5 specification clearly defines which elements do and do not have contents.

Correctness

If you remember, XHTML is actually the better way to go. It has more rules and more examination, and thus gives the spelling `<br/>` preference (in the sense of being better). Unfortunately, this is no longer true. HTML5 defined empty elements very clearly, and it indicated which ones are not closed with a slash. Using this spelling, it's not certain that valid XHTML will be created, since there's more to it than just that

(XML head fields, attributes. etc.). It is thus perfectly senseless and makes viewing the document more difficult. If you regard a cutout, the impression is formed that it concerns XHTML. However, that is not the case and begins an unfortunate chain of errors. Developers who do not know HTML might nevertheless be irritated by specific tags on other sites that do not appear to be closed. In addition, here it must be said that people, having access to the source code of HTML, should learn it themselves rather than rely on protected bases of crude measures.

In earlier times, XML was used because editors could deal with it better. Current development environments such as Visual Studio are rather good in their HTML knowledge and need no private tutoring anymore.

Special Cases

Actually, there is only one correct special case: `<script></script>`. All the other ones are, at best, annoying.

The script tag can be empty if it only refers to one script file. However, then it may not be shortened. Thus, the following is correct:

```
1  <script src="my-script.js"></script>
```

The short spelling is consistently ignored by all other browsers on the market:

```
1  <script src="my-script.js" />
1  <script>
2  function ShowMe(v){
3    alert(v);
4  }
5  </script>
```

The reason for this is the XHTML specification. Here the pattern will be specified that an element cannot be empty. That is logical, because you can write script code directly into a tag.

Site Structure

Listing 3-1 shows the basic structure of a complete HTML site.

Listing 3-1. Structure of an HTML Site

```
1  <!DOCTYPE html>
2
3  <html lang="en" xmlns="http://www.w3.org/1999/xhtml">
4    <head>
5      <meta charset="utf-8" />
6      <title>Name</title>
7    </head>
```

```
8     <body>
9        Inhalt
10    </body>
11   </html>
```

The <body> tag indicates the contents range, the <head> tag is the control block. The HTML site can be regarded as a Document Object Model (DOM).

ℹ **DOM**   The Document Object Model (DOM) is a specification of an interface for access to HTML or XML documents.

In the browser, DOM is at your disposal via a JavaScript API. The contents range, so basically the <body> tag works as *document* object.

The Doctype

Each document must begin with information about the type of document. The browser recognizes by the Doctype declaration which type the HTML document is.

```
1    <!doctype    html>
```

The <head> element is a mandatory element and contains information about the document following the HTML body. See Listing 3-2.

Listing 3-2. Head Area of an HTML Site

```
1    <!doctype html>
2    <head>
3      <meta charset="utf-8">
4      <meta name="viewport"
5           content="width=device-width, initial-scale=1.0">
6      <meta name="keywords"
7           content="Diese Angaben können weggelassen werden">
8      <link rel="stylesheet" href="style.css">
9      <style>
10       <!--- Platz für CSS  -->
11     </style>
12     <title>Meine erste HTML5-Seite</title>
13   </head>
```

Codings

You should always specify the encoding you need explicitly. UTF-8 is the most important standard, since it contains all the special characters and Asian characters.

ⓘ As example, in old HTML documents you had to write down umlauts as ü, ä, etc. in order for them to be represented. These so-called entities are no longer necessary, unless you cannot use UTF-8 (for whatever reason).

In order to prevent web pages from being viewed in a very small format on your mobile phone, you can indicate scaling with <meta name="viewport"…>, which adapts the site to the viewport. This representation control and the associated document features are discussed in detail in Chapter 4 on CSS.

The other meta-information such as author, keywords, and description are automatically ignored by search engines such as Google and can be omitted.

The title shows the names of the file in the browser or the tabs and should therefore be meaningful. Consider a single page application, which can be provided with AngularJS and can be used across multiple pages.

HTML5 Site Structure

Listing 3-3 shows typical HTML5 coding for a page.

Listing 3-3. Typical HTML5 Page

```
1    <!doctype html>
2    <html>
3    <head>
4      <meta charset="utf-8">
5      <title>HTML5-Seite mit Grundstruktur</title>
6    </head>
7
8    <body>
9      <header>
10       <img src="logo.png" alt="logo">
11       <h1>My Company</h1>
12     </header>
13
14     <footer>
15       <a href="contact.html">Kontakt</a>
16       <p>&copy;  2016 by Joerg Krause</p>
17     </footer>
18   </body>
19   </html>
```

The <body> is the visible range of the web page. Most web pages have a so-called page header that appears before the body and usually contains a logo, title, and navigation elements.

Further there is the element called <footer> that should contain the contact, imprint, copyright, and possibly the sitemap. Although the name suggests it's a position below the contents, this is not necessary. This concerns a semantic element; it's not an organization regulation.

Listing 3-4. Structure of Navigation

```
1    <body>
2      <header>
3        <img src="logo.gif" alt="logo">
4        <h1>Heading</h1>
5        <nav>
6          <ul>
7            <li><a href="#link_1.html">Wiki</a></li>
8            <li><a href="#link_2.html">Blog</a></li>
9            <li><a href="#link_3.html">Forum</a></li>
10         </ul>
11       </nav>
12     </header>
```

The navigation is enclosed by a new <nav> element, which can also be used for the under navigation.

Think about placing the navigation at the end of the document. You can then absolutely position it in the header and get a pleasing representation on mobile devices.

During a placement before the document's contents, you can mark the contents with the <main role="Main"> tag in order to let screen readers jump directly to the page contents.

Listing 3-5. Structure of Sections

```
1    <!doctype html>
2    <html>
3    <head>
4      <meta charset="utf-8">
5      <title>HTML5 Page with Base Structure</title>
6    </head>
7
```

```
 8   <body>
 9     <header>
10       <img src="logo.gif" alt="logo">
11       <h1>Title</h1>
12     </header>
13
14     <main role="main">
15       <h1>Heading</h1>
16       <p>This is my first HTML5 page</p>
17       ... more content
18     </main>
19
20     <aside>
21       <h2>More links</h2>
22       <ul>
23         <li><a href="link_1.html">Wiki</a></li>
24         <li><a href="link_2.html">Blog</a></li>
25         <li><a href="link_3.html">Forum</a></li>
26       </ul>
27     </aside>
28
29     <footer>
30     </footer>
31   </body>
32 </html>
```

Sidebars or marginal notes are represented in HTML5 by the <aside> element. It doesn't matter where the sidebar will be placed (right or left or down the side), because you'll determine that later with specific CSS features. The <aside> block contains information about the contents about the web page; however, they aren't automatically part of the content of the web page. Also, this is a semantic element.

Listing 3-6. Contents Range of a Simple HTML Site

```
 1   <!doctype html>
 2   <html>
 3   <head>
 4     <meta charset="utf-8">
 5     <title>HTML5 Page</title>
 6   </head>
 7
 8   <body>
 9     <header>
10       <img src="logo.gif" alt="logo">
11       <h1>Title</h1>
12     </header>
13
```

```
14    <article>
15      <h1>Heading</h1>
16      <p>This is my first HTML5 page</p>
17      ... more content
18    </article>
19
20    <aside>
21      <section>
22        <h2>Contact</h2>
23        <ul>
24          <li><a href="link_1.html">Wiki</a></li>
25          <li><a href="link_2.html">Blog</a></li>
26          <li><a href="link_3.html">Forum</a></li>
27        </ul>
28      </section>
29
30      <section>
31      <h2>More links</h2>
32      <ul>
33        <li><a href="link_1.html">Wiki</a></li>
34        <li><a href="link_2.html">Blog</a></li>
35        <li><a href="link_3.html">Forum</a></li>
36      </ul>
37      </section>
38    </aside>
39
40    <footer>
41    </footer>
42    </body>
43    </html>
```

For the distinction of the contents range, there are three elements:

- <main>: The main content of the site.

- <article>: An article that contains a heading (and possibly some sections, closed in on itself, and a header and footer)

- <section>: A section like a chapter, a...

Use <article> if contents in the one paragraph are final. Use <section> if there are several similar blocks.

ℹ The actual content in the examples in this chapter do not really matter. It's the structure that matters here.

Elements of the Page

Contents of an HTML site are text, text elements, and external resources such as pictures and videos.

ℹ️ This section is only a compact overview of the possibilities for beginners, in order to set the stage. You are encouraged to check out the complete documentation if you have questions and need more guidance. A good starting point is W3Schools at http://www.w3schools.com/.

Text Elements

Under text structuring, all the elements are summarized, which reflects the structure of the text of a web page. For example, headings or text sales.

- `<h1>` … `<h6>`: Headings in six hierarchical levels
- `<p>`: Text paragraphs
- `<pre>`: Preformatted text
- `<blockquote>`: Quotation blocks
- `<figure>`: Graphic additions, about charts, code examples, and photos
- `<figcaption>`: Description of the contents of one `<figure>` element
- `<hr>`: Thematic break, a horizontal line
- `<ol>`: Regulatory lists (with numbers/letters)
- `<ul>`: Unordered lists (enumerating characters)
- `<li>`: Elements that have created lists with `<ol>` and/or `<ul>`
- `<dl>`: Definition lists
- `<dt>`: Term that's described in a description list
- `<dd>`: Closer representations of `<dt>`; definition data
- `<div>`: Grouping element without a semantic meaning

All these elements are block elements, so they stand without further measures alone on a line. The following elements fall on the free range under block elements.

Headings (h1 ... h6)

The headings (h = heading) are always shown in bold and have simply a different size to be distinguished, as shown in Figure 3-3.

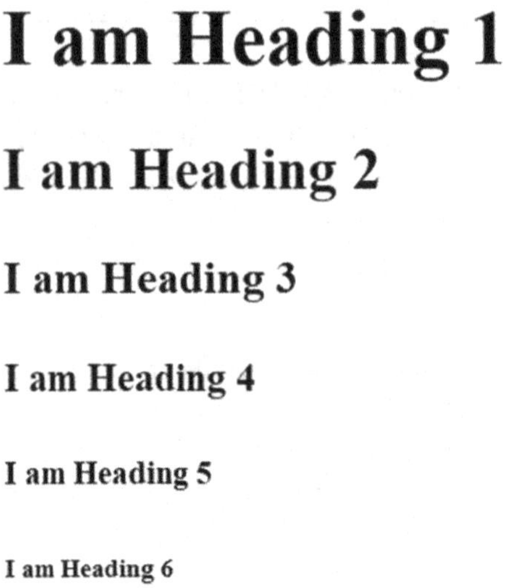

I am Heading 1

I am Heading 2

I am Heading 3

I am Heading 4

I am Heading 5

I am Heading 6

Figure 3-3. *Various headings*

```
1    <h1>Here we go</h1>
2    <h2>Headings are not nested</h2>
```

Paragraphs (p)

Paragraphs (p = paragraph) are blocks of text.

```
1    <p>A paragraph.</p>
```

Preformatted (pre)

Normally the renderer removes them when it notices extra blanks (only one blank is rendered) and ignores all other spaces and line breaks. If these are needed nevertheless, you can use the preformatted (pre = preformatted) tag.

The blockquote Tag

Quotation blocks are engaged and formatted in a block.

The figure and figcaption Tags

This is a general form for figures. It is used for graphic charts, code examples, photos, and so on. <figcaption> describes the contents of the image, or rather of a <figure> element.

```
1   <figure>
2       <img src="joerg.jpg" alt="Joerg Is A Geek" width="100" height="20\
3   0">
4       <figcaption>The Author</figcaption>
5   </figure>
```

The hr Tag

This is a thematic break, a horizontal line.

The ol and li Tags

These tags create regulatory lists (ol = ordered list, with numbers/letters). Each element of the list is based on the <li> tag (listing item). Lists can be interlocked.

The ul and li Tags

These tags format unordered lists (ul = unordered list, with enumerating characters). Each element of the list is based on the <li> tag (an unordered item). Lists can be interlocked.

```
1   <ul>
2     <li>HTML</li>
3     <li>CSS</li>
4     <li>JavaScript</li>
5   </ul>
```

The dl, dt, and dd Tags

Description lists (DL = description list) contain two elements—the expression (dt = definition term) and the definition of the expression (dd = definition data).

The div Tag

This is a grouping element without any semantic meaning.

Text Flow

Elements in the flow text stand like letters in lines and displace the following elements only from their own area.

- `<a>`: A reference goal with the attribute name

- `<b>`, `<em>`, `<i>`, `<kbd>`, `<mark>`, `<s>`, `<small>`, `<strong>`, `<sub>`, `<sup>`, and `<u>`: Formats such as fat, cursive, marked, high, and down.

- `<cite>`, `<q>`: Quotations

- `<dfn>`, `<abbr>`: Definitions and abbreviations

- `<code>`, `<var>`, and `<samp>`: Semantic emphases

- `<time>`: Time or date

- `<ruby>`, `<rt>`, and `<rp>`: Supplemental information on Asian characters

- `<bdi>` and `<bdo>`: Temporary change of the river direction.

- `<br>` and `<wbr>`: Line breaks

- `<del>` and `<ins>`: Change markings with weak semantic meaning

- `<span>`: Grouping element without semantic meaning

References

- `<a>`: The anchor tag, with which hyperlinks are provided

- `<map>` and `<area>`: Clickable ranges in pictures or a freely defined structure

```
1   <img src="planets.gif" width="145" height="126" alt="Planets"
2    usemap="#planetmap">
3
4   <map name="planetmap">
5      <area shape="rect" coords="0,0,82,126" href="sun.htm" alt="Sun">
6      <area shape="circle" coords="90,58,3" href="mercur.htm" alt="Merc\
7   ury">
8      <area shape="circle" coords="124,58,8" href="venus.htm" alt="Venu\
9   s">
10  </map>
```

Tables

The following tags format information into a tabular format:

- `<table>`: Table element
- `<caption>`: Heading outside of the table
- `<col>` and `<colgroup>`: Column definitions
- `<thead>`, `<tbody>`, and `<tfoot>`: Area definitions (head, contents, and foot)
- `<tr>`: Arrays
- `<th>`, `<td>`: Head element in a row and/or data element in a row

```
1   <table>
2      <thead>
3      <tr>
4         <th>Month</th>
5         <th>Revenues</th>
6      </tr>
7      </thead>
8      <tfoot>
9      <tr>
10        <td>Total</td>
11        <td>$ 180</td>
12     </tr>
13     </tfoot>
14     <tbody>
15     <tr>
16        <td>January</td>
17        <td>$ 100</td>
18     </tr>
19     <tr>
20        <td>February</td>
21        <td>$ 210</td>
22     </tr>
23     </tbody>
24  </table>
```

Multimedia and Graphics

The following tags format multimedia and graphics on a web page:

- `<img>` and `<picture>`: General picture and/or alternative source of a picture with a Media Query (see Chapter 4)
- `<canvas>`: 2D indication surface for script-steered pictures

- `<svg>`: Indication surface for vector graphics

- `<math>`: Zone for mathematical formulas

- `<iframe>`, `<embed>`, `<object>`, and `<param>`: Embedded data and sites

- `<audio>`, `<video>`, `<source>`, and `<track>`: Embedded media and their elements

```
1  <canvas id="myCanvas"></canvas>
2
3  <script>
4  var canvas = document.getElementById("myCanvas");
5  var ctx = canvas.getContext("2d");
6  ctx.fillStyle = "#FF0000";
7  ctx.fillRect(0, 0, 80, 80);
8  </script>
```

Forms

The following tags format information that's presented in forms:

- `<form>`: Form with sending off references

- `<fieldset>` and `<legend>`: Section (group) in the form

- `<label>`: Field identifier

- `<datalist>`: List for a combo box

- `<input>`: Universal input field

- `<button>`: Button

- `<select>`, `<optgroup>`, and `<option>`: Folding menu (drop-down) or box

- `<textarea>`: Text entry box of several lines

- `<keygen>`: Key generator (only Chrome/Firefox)

- `<output>`, `<progress>`, and `<meter>`: Various output formats for values and/or measured values

```
1  <input list="countries">
2
3  <datalist id="countries">
4     <option value="Germany">
5     <option value="Netherland">
6     <option value="France">
```

```
 7      <option value="Denmark">
 8      <option value="Austria">
 9         ...
10    </datalist>
```

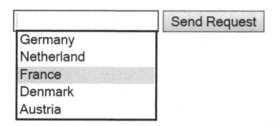

Figure 3-4. *Combo box with a data list*

Scripts

- `<script></script>`: Load script or use it directly

This tag always requires a closing tag, even if it does not have any content. This is because the parser just looks for the closing tag because the content is treated as text and may contain any sort of "tag-like" parts as part of the script. Hence the parser cannot treat that part as a regular structure in HTML.

Interactive Elements

The following tags are used with interactive elements:

- `<details>` and `<summary>`: Explanation of contents

- `<dialog>`:

- `<menu>`, `<menuitem>`, and `<command>`:

General and Universal Attributes

Universal attributes have a firm meaning in all the elements in which they occur. There are however deviations concerning the elements, in which the universal attributes may occur. Universal attributes can occur within `<body>` elements, thus they can be in most elements. The actual usability of the element is inferred from an HTML reference. Universal attributes are:

- `id`

- `class`

- accesskey

- contextmenu

- contenteditable

- data--Attributes

- itemprop--Micro data

The id Attribute

The id attribute identifies an element within a document. It predominantly serves as a goal for the links within the site, and as identifier within the CSS selectors or as identifier for JavaScript. Contents of the id attribute must be the only thing in the document.

```
1   <div id="footnote-collection">
```

The name for id has to begin with a letter and contains as many other indications as desired, out of [A-Za-z0-9_:-]. It is permitted in all elements except: base, head, HTML, meta, script, styles, and headlines. These elements are not addressable, because they are not part of the DOM or can only exist once.

The class Attribute

The attribute class is not an empty character string without blanks. It is permitted in all elements except: base, head, HTML, meta, script, styles, and headlines. The class attribute assigns an element to one or more classes. Classes serve to mark homogenous elements in the markup with the goal of being able to select them. It does not have to be homogenous elements.

Classes are typically used for CSS or as a selector for JavaScript. Other processes can recognize such elements on the basis of the class.

⚠ Abuse of Class   Very often classes are used as universal tools for the selection of elements. The use should be limited, however, to style templates; that is, they should serve the selection of CSS. If you need universal selectors, the data attributes in HTML5 are suitable for this job.

The example in Listing 3-7 shows how classes are used. You can check out the details about CSS in Chapter 4.

Listing 3-7. Site with Styles

```
1    <style>
2
3      .warning {
4        color: red;
5      }
6      p.warning {
7        border: 1px solid red;
8        background-color: peachpuff;
9      }
10
11   </style>
12   <body>
13     <h1 class="warning">Warning</h1>
14
15     <p class="warning">Read more books!</p>
16
17     <p><strong class="warning">Attention:</strong> Learn HTML!</p>
18   </body>
```

The example classifies all elements with the text color red. The paragraph with the class warning is provided additionally with a red edge and a skin colored background.

The accesskey Attribute

With accesskey, you can set key combination on the keyboard, which the users can press in order to have elements start directly. Its implementation in each browser is different. Likewise, it can happen that shortcuts are already occupied by browser menus.

The accesskey attribute has further disadvantages. These begin with other functions or with the concept of the keyboard operation of web contents, up to missing standards for the allocation of links. There is no generally accepted convention as to which keyboard shortcut should be used for which function, links, etc. Such "standards" are discussed among specialists again and again, and the concept of accesskey attributes is not practical in HTML. The concept of shortcuts in future HTML specifications will nevertheless have to be considered.

The contenteditable Attribute

The contenteditable attribute specifies whether you edit contents of an element (changes) or not. The possible values are true or false (the latter is the standard).

```
1    <section contenteditable="true">
2      <h2>The heading might be changed.</h2>
3      <p>This para can be changed.</p>
4    </section>
```

The `section` element has the universal attribute `contenteditable` with the value true. Since the elements `<h2>` and `<p>` haven't set an attribute, the editing capability isn't activated.

The contextmenu Attribute

The `contextmenu` attribute specifies whether you can open a context menu with the right mouse button or not.

```
1   <body contextmenu="info">
2     <menu type="context" id="info">
3       <menu label="info">
4         <menuitem label="Joerg"
5   onclick="window.open('http://www.joergkrause.de');">\
6   </menuitem>
7           <menuitem label="IT-Visions"
8                     onclick="window.open('http://www-it-visions.de');"><\
9   /menuitem>
10        </menu>
11      </menu>
12  </body>
```

⚠ **Support**   At present, the `contextmenu` attribute works only with Edge and Mozilla Firefox. Neither Chrome nor Safari have incorporated this procedure.

The dir Attribute

The `dir` attribute defines the writing direction within the document. Languages such as Hebrew and Arabic are written from right to left. However, in the Unicode System, the information about the writing direction is already there. Use this element if you must control an element's writing direction. CSS has additional possibilities to check the writing direction.

```
1   <q dir="rtl"/> <q<
```

The value is set by using one of these character sequences: `ltr` or `rtl` (left to right or right to left).

It is permitted in all elements except: `applet`, `base`, `basefont`, `br`, `frame`, `frame set`, `HR`, `iframe`, `param`, and `script`.

The draggable Attribute

The draggable attribute determines whether an element with the drag and drop can be dragged by the API.

- true: The element can be drawn and shifted

- false: The element cannot be drawn and shifted

The dropzone Attribute

The dropzone attribute specifies whether an element can be moved, copied, or linked when it's pulled with drag and drop.

The hidden Attribute

The hidden attribute shows that an element is not longer relevant and is therefore faded out. You should never use the hidden attribute to hide contents, because users can easily view the text from the source code.

⚠ **No Protection!**   Using the hidden attribute doesn't give your data any genuine protection. The data is visible in the source text of the site, which is easily accessed in most browsers.

The lang Attribute

The lang attribute sets (https://www.iana.org/) a specific language setting, and the following element contents firmly. The attribute should also be defined with monolingual documents in the root element (HTML) and for multilingual documents in each element, starting from where the language change takes place.

```
1    <html lang="de">
```

The contents are IANA-language shortcuts. It is permitted in all elements except: applet, base, basefont, br, frame, frame set, HR, iframe, meta, param, and script.

Always use the language attribute in the HTML tag, in order to indicate the language of the text on your site. For sites that are delivered as XML, use the xml: lang attribute instead.

The spellcheck Attribute

The spellcheck attribute specifies whether the browser's internal spell checker is to be activated or not. The value can be either true or false. You can use this attribute in the following elements: inputs and textarea.

Spell Checker   The spell checker uses the "natural" language of the browser. Often this depends on the operating system. For users who are somewhat bilingual, this can be annoying. Usually switching this off is helpful. If an editor field has a spell checker, it should really be used and you look for a commercial component with programmable features.

The style Attribute

The style attribute's content is CSS code. Normally you note CSS in your own CSS files. For some purposes it is however meaningful to note style rules directly in the element, for example, if many pictures on a map are placed and the positions to be determined are directly where they're supposed to be. Some people call this an *inline style*. Compared to the noted variants, this can be restrictive. Definitions of pseudo-attributes and the context of medium are not possible. You should use the style attribute only in justified exceptions.

```
1   <img src="" style="left:247px; top:83px">
```

This attribute is allowed for all elements except: base, basefont, head, HTML, meta, param, script, styles, and headlines.

The tabindex Attribute

The tabindex attribute makes it possible, with the help of the tab key, to start arbitrary elements of an HTML file. The operation with the keyboard complements the attribute accesskey, but it's by far more robust and globally supported where the keyboard is present.

The title Attribute

The title attribute describes an element. Browsers show descriptive text when the user points toward it with the mouse. This is also called a *tool hint*. Commentating from links is typical, supplying additional information to pictures or the explanation abbreviations. Calling should be economically implemented on superordinate elements.

```
1   <a href="http://example.org" title="external link">
```

Additional information, which is not immediately evident from the `href` attribute, is shown in the `title` attribute.

```
1    <abbr title="International Panel for Climate Change">IPCC</abbr>
```

Abbreviations are described using the `title` attribute.

The attribute is allowed for all elements except: `basefont`, `head`, `HTML`, `meta`, `param`, `script`, `styles`, and `headlines`.

⚠ Browser Behavior   Browsers represent contents such as `title` attributes differently. Firefox writes about only one line. Internet Explorer shows, if necessary, a field of several lines. Avoid very long text and radical changes. They can stand out and will need the assistance of CSS contents and attributes.

CHAPTER 4

CSS: Cascading Style Sheets

CSS—Cascading Style Sheets—is a layout and formatting language that enables you to format markup languages such as HTML. Ideally the HTML document contains only semantic information and, with CSS, these will be formatted formatively and typographically.

HTML provides some basic formatting, like larger point sizes with headings. These can be adapted to CSS, just as all not formatted elements can be formatted. Format tags in HTML and format attributes should not be used in principle anymore. They became outdated since HTML5. CSS is now used in their place.

With CSS, it's also possible to separately specify output modes for different media, such as a monitor (screen), projection, and print.

Figure 4-1. *Logo for CSS3*

© Jörg Krause 2016
J. Krause, *Introducing Web Development*, DOI 10.1007/978-1-4842-2499-1_4

CSS Basics

A HTML document consists of semantically meaningful awards for headings, sales, lists, etc. The instructions for CSS must be placed in such a way that the browser can assign these to the elements. In addition, these instructions must be written somewhere. There are three main options:

- The style attribute, which every HTML element knows

- The <style></style> element, which summarizes several styles

- The <link /> element, which refers to a file that contains several style definitions

The preferential way is the use of a CSS file. The browser can buffer these files in the cache and the content can be made smaller with appropriate tools, so that you save range (not because of the range, but because of the associated achievement gain).

Local style elements should be used only in exceptional cases, in order to make short-term changes to complex files. Such local instructions for style have a higher priority. The style attribute extends or modifies the styles for only one element. It has the highest priority over contradictory rules from local or imported styles.

The link containing the CSS file takes place in the HEAD range of the HTML document:

```
1   <link rel="stylesheet"
2         type="text/css"
3         href="styles/style.css">
```

Note that the path of the file has to be indicated relative to the HTML document.

CSS Syntax

CSS syntax is quite simple. The essential structure consists of two components:

- Selector

- Rule set

The *selector* determines to which element the rules refer.

```
1   Selector {
2       Rule set
3   }
```

If the styles are within the style attributes, then they are only valid for the specified element. Here the selector is therefore not applicable.

However, the rule set consists of rules. These are written in the following form:

```
Style: Parameter;
```

The semicolon at the end is necessary.

The Selector Component

The selector is constituted so that elements on the side will purposefully be reached. The entire pattern of the selectors is rather comprehensive. Here, the most important components are shown at first.

Elements (Tags)

With CSS you can address individual elements. The syntax in looks as follows:

```
TagName { Rule set }
```

If you want to reach all <p> elements, it's enough to write the following:

```
p { }
```

IDs

Frequently only one tag is changed. The addressed tag must be identifiable as such, which means it has to be attainable with an ID. The HTML attribute of the same name contains a character sequence, which is attainable in the CSS characteristics. An ID can only be used to add an element within a document, therefore it should occur only once. The syntax looks as follows:

```
#id { }
```

Here's an example of a button:

```
1  <style>
2  #send {
3    color: red;
4  }
5  </style>
6  <button id="send">Send</button>
```

Classes

More frequently, several elements need to be addressed. In addition, you can address server classes, which are written into the attribute class as HTML. You can hand this attribute several classes separated by spaces and combine the rule sets. This saves extensive work. Bootstrap uses this to provide many modification options with a few basic rule sets. Contrary to IDs, the same class for several elements can be defined and may then occur in several documents.

The syntax looks as follows:

```
.class { }
```

Here's an example of a button:

```
1  <style>
2  .btn {
3    color: red;
4  }
5  </style>
6  <button class="btn">Send</button>
```

Attributes

Attributes of HTML elements can be referred to using the following syntax:

```
[name] { }
```

```
[name="wert"] { }
```

Here's another example of a button:

```
1  <style>
2  [data-item] {
3    color: blue;
4  }
5  </style>
6  <a href="link.html" data-item="22">Continue</button>
```

If the value of the attribute (to right of the equals character) is not indicated, then the existence of the attribute is considered as sufficient to use the rules.

Logical Selection

It often occurs that rule sets apply to several selectors. In addition a logical OR is needed, which is represented by a comma in CSS:

```
a, b { }
```

There is no connection between a and b, so the rule is independently applied to both. The placeholders a and b in the example can be more complex selectors.

More Selectors

In practice, these selectors are not sufficient. Table 4-1 is a compact overview of all the other forms.

Table 4-1. *Simple CSS Selectors*

Symbol	Description
*	Universal
tag	Element
.class	Class (Attribute class)
#id	ID (Attribute ID)
[a]	Attribute is present
[a=v]	Attribute value
[a~=v]	Attribute contains value as word
[a|=v]	Attribute does not contains value
[a^=v]	Attribute starts with
[a$=v]	Attribute ends with
[a*=v]	Attribute contains value

Handling hierarchies is essential, because HTML documents are hierarchies, often referred to as trees. Figure 4-2 shows the relationship between elements in the document tree.

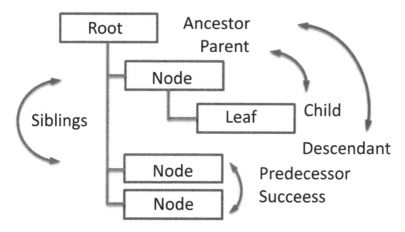

Figure 4-2. *Elements in the hierarchy of a HTML site*

Table 4-2 shows the syntax for CSS.

Table 4-2. *CSS Selectors for Hierarchies*

Symbol	Description
e > f	Selection if f is a child of e
e f	Selection if f is an immediate successor to e
e + f	Selection if f is a successor to e
e ~ f	Selection if f is a sibling of e

In this case, the use of predecessors and parents is missing as a function. You can get this result by exchanging the elements.

Pseudo-selectors do not have a comparable representation in HTML, but result from the position of elements or the use. There are three kinds of such selectors:

- Static positions

- Selection of ranges

- Dynamic behavior

Table 4-3. *Static CSS Selectors*

Symbol	Description
::first-line	First line
::first-letter	First letter
::before	Before the element
::after	After the element
::selection	The selected text

Table 4-4. *CSS Selectors for Ranges*

Symbol	Description
:root	Basic element
:empty	Applies only if the item is empty
:first-child	The first child element of a list
:last-child	The last child element of a list
:nth-child()	A particular child element of a list
:nth-last-child()	A particular child element at the end of a list

(continued)

Table 4-4. (*continued*)

Symbol	Description
:only-child	Valid only when there is only one child element
:first-of-type	First child element of a type
:last-of-type	Last child element of a type
:nth-of-type()	Child element of a type in a list
:nth-last-of-type()	Child element of a type at the end of a list
:only-of-type	Only this type from a list

Table 4-5. *Dynamic CSS Selectors*

Symbol	Description
:link	A hyperlink
:visited	A hyperlink that has already been visited
:hover	A hyperlink to the hovering the mouse
:active	A hyperlink that is active (clicked)
:focus	An item that has the focus (blinking cursor)
:target	An item that has a target attribute
:disabled	An item that is disabled (disabled attribute)
:enabled	An item that is enabled (not disabled attribute)
:checked	An item that is checked (a check box)
:valid	An element that is valid
:invalid	An element that is not valid
:lang()	An item that the appropriate lang="" attribute
:not()	Negates the following selections (this is an operator)

The examination of the validity of form elements presupposes that the attributes defined in HTML5 are used, such as max length, required , DATE , e-mail, etc.

Contrary to the long attribute, the long() in CSS can determine a fallback, thus de-DE reacts to de, etc.

⚠ **Browser Support**   Not all the current browsers support all of these pseudo-classes. Check the online documentation of the appropriate browsers before you use any of these classes, for best results.

The Box Model

HTML supports two kinds of description forms for elements—flow elements and block elements. *Flow elements* embed themselves in text. These elements do not have dimensions such as width and height, because they depend on the surrounding elements. *Block elements*, however, have dimensions and displace any adjacent elements when necessary. This displacement behavior is adaptable, and is up to the intended overlay. Using special rules, you can change these elements, which are actually flow elements, into block elements. This also works in reverse.

The box model of the block element defines characteristics for almost all the ranges of a rectangular range (see Figure 4-3).

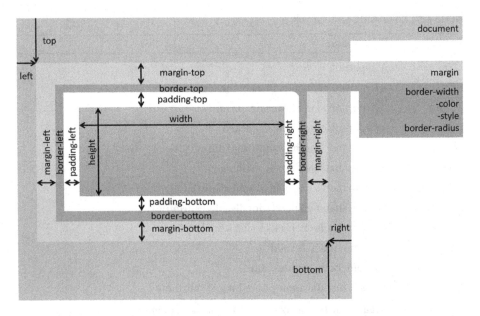

Figure 4-3. *Components of the box model*

It's important to recognize that the instructions of width and height are not the final measurements, but indicate the dimensions of the contents. If a framework encloses the box, the final width of the frameworks must be computed again. If the framework on all sides is alike:

Width = edge * 2 + framework width * 2 + distance * 2 Height = edge * 2 + framework width * 2 + distance * 2

If there's a difference with the edges, calculating the framework widths and distances becomes accordingly more complex.

Components of the Box

Each component of the box has its own separate value. The internal range includes the contents. The components are:

- padding: The internal distance
- border: The framework on the outside
- margin: The outside edge, the distance to other elements

Since the box is associated with a rectangle, four values have to be indicated:

- top
- right
- bottom
- left

Counting Method   The origin can be seen on screens and printed pages in the upper-left corner. In some rules, several values can be directly indicated. In such cases, the four values shown in order are interpreted, beginning with top (upper-left) and then further in the clockwise direction.

With margin, horizontally formed distances are valid. However, the vertical distances can collapse under certain circumstances (collapsed). This occurs if neither frameworks (border) nor distance (padding) are used without exemption (clear). The lower edge of the upper box with the top margin of the lower box is then overlaid. If the edges are of various sizes, the wider edge will be used.

Exceptions   There is a whole set of exceptions from the unification rules of the edges. Consult the official documentation for example of more complex sites.

The Box Model in CSS3

CSS3 introduced an extension of the box model, and it allows a more flexible assignment. With help from the characteristic box-sizing, it's possible to specify where width and height are used. Thereby one of the following indications is allowed:

- content-box: Default value, information is valid only for contents
- padding-box: Information is valid for contents and interior distances

- border-box: Information is valid for contents, interior distances, and framework

- inherit: box-sizing of the parents element takes over (inheritance)

Attention of Media

CSS allows you to specify the representation of a document for a different edition media. The allocation of stylesheets to a medium takes place using media queries.

A list with criteria is called media inquiry, and it must fulfill an edition medium, so that a stylesheet is merged for processing. Medium inquiries consist of a type of medium (e.g., screen or printer), a medium characteristic (e.g., color rendition), or a combination of both. Stylesheets can be tailored to a variety of edition media.

 Media queries cannot be noted in the style attributes.

Syntax

The medium type takes place as a simple keyword, for example screen.

> If no medium inquiry is indicated or if the indicated inquiry consists only of blanks, then the default value is valid (all).

Listing 4-1. Medium Inquiry in an HTML Document

```
1   <link rel="stylesheet" href="monitor.css" media="screen">
2   <link rel="stylesheet" href="printer.css" media="print">
```

The print type ensures that the stylesheet printer.css is used during the printout. On a screen, however, monitor.css will be activated.

 This approach has the disadvantage that both stylesheets often contain the same CSS rules. On top of that, at least two files are needed.

You can also omit the media attribute, at which point the stylesheet is valid for all media. In the alternative file, only the changes must be noted.

Listing 4-2. Medium Inquiry with a Standard Document

```
1   <link rel="stylesheet" href="monitor.css">
2   <link rel="stylesheet" href="printer.css" media="print">
```

The rules can also be accommodated in the CSS file, as shown in Listing 4-3.

Listing 4-3. Rules for Printing

```
1   @media print {
2       /* Regeln für Druckausgabe */
3   }
```

Media have certain characteristics, which modify the selection of the rule. With the screen type, this can be the number of pixels, for example. Prefixes like min and max permit you to indicate a range.

```
1   <link rel="stylesheet" href="pt.css"
2         media="(orientation: portrait)">
```

The stylesheet pt.css is merged if the content of the sites is in the portrait format.

```
1   <style type="text/css" media="(color)">
2       /* Farbangaben. */
3   </style>
```

The style element indicates any color information, if the display can represent colors. A black-and-white printer would profit from the fact that no poorly readable colors are used (yellow and white for example).

```
1   @import 'layout.css' (min-width: 150mm);
```

The stylesheet layout.css is used if the normal range of the medium amounts to 150mm at least.

Medium inquiries can be grouped with logical ORs. As is the case with the CSS selectors, the comma is used. Grouped inquiries are completely independent from each other. As soon as at least one of the inquiries applies, the declarations are used.

```
1   @media print, embossed {
2       /* Formate für Printmedien. */
3   }
```

In this example, a stylesheet is specified, and it can be used for both the print and embossed types.

Several medium characteristics can be connected using the and keyword. A stylesheet is processed only if all its associated criteria is fulfilled.

```
1  @media (min-width: 130mm) and (max-width: 160mm) {
2    /* Kompaktes Layout */
3  }
4  @media print and (color), screen and (color) {
5    /* Farbangaben */
6  }
```

The style element indicates any color information, assuming the edition medium can represent colors. If a type of medium is noted at the beginning of the medium inquiry, then this information can be placed in front of only or can use the keyword emergency. only hides the medium inquiry in browsers that do not support them. Otherwise, the inquiry is processed as if the keyword was missing. If the operator is placed in front of not, the inquiry is denied.

```
1  @media only all and (min-width: 150mm) {
2    /* Layout */
3  }
4  @media not all and (monochrome) {
5    /* Farben */
6  }
```

This example shows how screens that are at least 150mm wide are assigned to the range rules. A browser that understands medium inquiries ignores the keyword only. Denying the inquiry monochrome enables you to use the color information by all media that can deal with color information.

Handling Units   A characteristic deals with relative length specifications like em or ex. When these values are processed, the default value of the browser is assumed, which was defined by the user. Normally, em refers to the current text, which is however not defined and on the level of the medium inquiry yet. You can find more about units at the end of this chapter.

Each characteristic can also be used without a declared value. In this case, CSS checks whether the characteristic on the used medium is present.

```
1  @media (width) {
2    /* Das Ausgabemedium besitzt das Merkmal "Breite" */
3  }
4  @media (color) {
5    /* Das Ausgabemedium besitzt das Merkmal "Farbfähigkeit" */
6  }
```

Parameters

The characteristic width determines the width of the normal range (viewport) with sequential media. With paged media, it determines the width of a side. The prefixes min and max can be used to indicate borders.

```
1  @media (width: 60em) {
2    /* Breite entspricht genau 60em */
3  }
4  @media (min-width: 50em) {
5    /* Breite beträgt mindestens 50em */
6  }
7  @media (max-width: 70em) {
8    /* Breite beträgt höchstens 70em */
9  }
```

With characteristics that assign themselves to the normal indicator, it's almost always meaningful to use one of the possible prefixes since the actual indicator width is not set by the user.

The characteristic height determines the height of the normal range (viewport) with sequential media; with paged media, it determines the height of a site. The prefixes min and max are used to indicate borders.

The device-width and device-height characteristics determine the width and height of the output device, for example, the width of a screen in pixels. The value is a positive length. The prefixes min and max can be used to indicate borders.

```
1  @media (device-width: 800px) {
2    /* Breite entspricht genau 800 Pixel */
3  }
4  @media (min-device-width: 800px) {
5    /* Breite beträgt mindestens 800px */
6  }
7  @media (max-device-width: 1024px) {
8    /* Breite beträgt höchstens 1024px */
9  }
```

⚠ Even if an output device possesses certain dimensions, that does not mean that the available range will be used. Likewise, the message of the pixels can deviate from the physical pixels, for example, in the case of retina displays. Likewise, not all devices announce their orientation by changing the values. On Apple devices, the width is always in portrait mode, even if the user turns the tablet around or uses it in horizontal format. Orientation must be likewise considered.

The orientation characteristic determines the page format of an edition medium. Orientation corresponds to the value landscape (landscape format), if the width value is larger than the height value. Otherwise, the orientation is set to portrait. The value is one of two keywords—portrait or landscape.

```
1   @media (orientation: portrait) {
2       /* Formate für hochformatige Ausgabemedien */
3   }
```

The aspect-ratio characteristic determines the relationship of the width characteristic to the height characteristic. The prefixes min and max can be used here.

```
1   @media (aspect-ratio: 4/3) { /* Fall 1 */ }
2   @media (min-aspect-ratio: 4/3) { /* Fall 2 */ }
3   @media (max-aspect-ratio: 4/3) { /* Fall 3 */ }
```

In this example, the relationship value 4/3 is assigned to the variant's "aspect ratio" of the characteristic. The stylesheet is processed if the aspect ratio of the normal range (viewport) corresponds exactly to 4 to 3 (case 1). That is that case with a normal range from 492 to 369 pixels. The stylesheet in case 2 is used, if the aspect ratio is 4/3 or more. In case 3, the stylesheet is processed only if the aspect ratio is smaller than 4/3 (for example, 2/3 or 1/3).

The device-aspect-ratio characteristic determines the relationship of the device-width characteristic to the deviceheight characteristic. This is implemented similar to the aspect-ratio characteristic

The color characteristic determines the number of bits that color equipment components (the red, green, or blue values) use. If the output device cannot show colors, the value 0 (zero) is applicable. For different color components, if a different number is used, then the lowest number of bits of the equipment counts. This value is a never a negative number.

```
1   @media (color: 2) { /* Einfaches Farblayout */ }
2   @media (min-color: 3) { /* Komplexes Farblayout */ }
3   @media (max-color: 2) { /* Einfaches Farblayout */ }
```

The color index characteristic determines the number of color definitions in the color chart of the edition medium. If the medium does not have a color chart, the value 0 (zero) is applicable. Usually only media possess a color chart.

```
1   @media (color-index: 16) {
2       /* genau 16 Farben stehen zur Verfügung */
3   }
4   @media (min-color-index: 20) {
5       /* Mindestens 20 Farben stehen zur Verfügung */
6   }
7   @media (max-color-index: 256) {
8       /* Höchstens 256 Farben stehen zur Verfügung */
9   }
```

Support for "color index" is at present not universal with all browsers.

The monochrome characteristic (black-and-white) determines the number of bits used to describe a black-and-white shade. If it does not concern equipment, which can represent only grayscale (but also colors), the value 0 (zero) is applicable

```
1   @media (monochrome: 1) {
2     /* only black and white are available */
3   }
4   @media (min-monochrome: 4) {
5     /* at least 16 shades of gray */
6   }
7   @media (max-monochrome: 8) {
8     /* a maximum of 256 shades of gray */
9   }
```

The light level characteristic determines the lightning conditions of the environment and this is determined by the brightness sensor of the camera. The following settings are possible:

- dim: Absorbed light only

- normal: The normal lighting level

- washed: Very bright, flooded with light. If the medium does not have a color chart, the value 0 (zero) is applicable. Usually only media possess a color chart, and the color rendition is reduced. To have a color chart, the value 0 (zero) is applicable. Usually only media possess a color chart, whose color rendition is reduced. The specification uses no firm lighting values, since many devices have their own contrast adjustments. The technologies are just too different (E-Ink remains legible in bright light, while crystal displays wouldn't support that). Since the brightness sensors are not frequently calibrated, the reaction is difficult to predict.

```
1    @media (light-level: normal) {
2      p {
3        background: url("texture.jpg");
4        color: #333 }
5    }
6    @media (light-level: dim) {
7      p {
8        background: #222;
9        color: #ccc }
10     }
```

```
11  @media (light-level: washed) {
12    p {
13      background: white;
14      color: black;
15      font-size: 2em; }
16  }
```

The pointer characteristic determines the accuracy of information that's entered as a point. It's often difficult to distinguish between touch devices, such as smartphones and tablets, with a mouse click, not to mention consoles such as the Wii. This is where you indicate touchpad or input pins. The following settings are possible:

- fine: For devices with mouse, touchpad, or input pins

- coarse: For devices with touch or gesture control

- none:

```
1  @media (pointer: coarse) {
2    input {
3      padding 1em;
4      font-size: 2em;
5    }
6  }
```

With touch devices, the font size and the interior distance of the input field are increased accordingly.

Since most devices have several input modes, and you don't know which method they will use at any one time, you can find out with any pointer whether there are input devices at all. You can't completely close specific devices with pointer or any-pointer. However, you can recognize (in combination with the display width) whether someone is using a smartphone, tablet, or desktop computer. Thus you can optimize web pages more exactly for certain devices.

The resolution characteristic determines the dissolution, thus the tightness, of the pixels on an edition medium. If the medium you're using does not use rectangular pixels (for example printers), then the characteristic can be used only in connection with a prefix. In this case, min-resolution determines the lowest possible inquiry, and max-resolution sets the highest possible tightness of the pixels.

```
1  @media (resolution: 96dpi) {
2    /* Die Auflösung beträgt 96 Bildpunkte pro Zoll */
3  }
4  @media (min-resolution: 200dpcm) {
5    /* Die Auflösung beträgt mindestens 200 Punkte pro cm */
6  }
7  @media (max-resolution: 300dpi) {
8    /* Die Auflösung beträgt höchstens 300 Punkte pro Zoll */
9  }
```

The scan characteristic determines the screen layout of output devices of the type tv. This can take place progressively and can corresponds, for instance, to the screen layout on a computer screen. If so, the value progressive applies. Or it can take place by line formation (i.e., individual character rows are gradually represented), in which case it applies the interlace value. The values are permitted as progressive or interlace.

```
1  @media (scan: progressive) {
2      /* screen layout */
3  }
```

The grid characteristic determines the raster characteristic of the edition media. With output devices, which represent contents in a raster, the value unity (1) usually applies; otherwise, you use the value zero (0).

```
1  @media (grid: 0) {
2      /* several font formattings */
3  }
```

The Viewport

The viewport indication is an HTML line that ensures that the web site is correctly rendered upon first call on mobile equipment.

The browsers of mobile devices often assume that the web sites aren't appropriate for them and that the web site width exceeds the display width. The browser viewport (normal range) is adjusted to 980 pixels wide, so that most web sites can be viewed completely. This has the disadvantage that the text ends up being very small and hard to read. The user must then zoom in in order to be able to read anything.

Viewport Configuration

The viewport code can be adapted very simply over an HTML element. If the web site deviates from the standard width, then you can adapt the viewport. Thus, you can ensure that the contents and the normal range agree. With these layouts, the web site is shown in the maximum size possible.

The starting view of apple.com zoomed on mobile devices (left) and cut out with readable text (right) is shown in Figure 4-4.

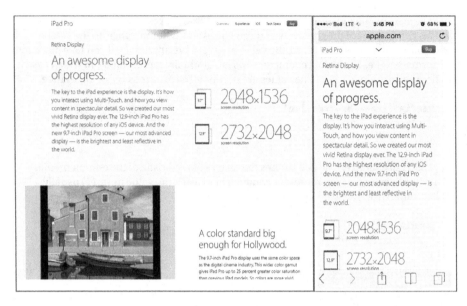

Figure 4-4. *Web site with and without zoom*

To make this change, you insert the following line into the head area of the site. This is then evaluated by the appropriate mobile devices.

```
1   <!DOCTYPE html>
2   <head>
3       <meta name="viewport" content="width=1024" />
4   </head>
5   <body>
6   </body>
```

If the web site in question is provided or optimized for mobile devices, you do not usually indicate a fixed width for the viewport. Smartphones have, for example, in the portrait format a logical width of 320px and in the landscape format 480px (physically, the value will be higher). This means that in the high and landscape format, the same contents, only in a different zoom shot level, would be shown.

Instead, you'll need to use a formula to convert this ratio suitably:

Width of the Viewports = Width of the Device

If the smartphone has a width of 320px in the portrait format, exactly 320px of the web site will be shown (1:1). Likewise, in the landscape format, 480px are shown. This flexible attitude is device-independent. On the other hand, it's possible to also use it in landscape format, which is beneficial.

The following comparison shows the effect. Figure 4-5 shows the site on a mobile phone with the meta element in the source code width=devicewidth (left) and without (right).

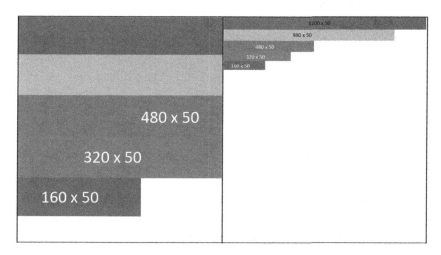

Figure 4-5. *With (left) and without (right) a meta element*

Viewport Configuration

The meta element for the viewport has further characteristics, apart from the width, which are formatted into a comma-separated list.

```
1  <meta name="viewport" content="width=device-width,
2                                 initial-scale=1.0,
3                                 user-scalable=no" />
```

- initial-scale: Specifies the initial zoom in degrees. 1.0 leads to the fact that the contents of 1:1 are represented, which is called a 320px-width diagram. The complete width on a screen with 320px wide fills it out (also shown in Figure 4-5). Accordingly, the 2x zoom leads to an enlargement by 2.0.

- user-scalable: You can define whether the user on the site can zoom (yes) or not (no).

- minimum-scale and maximum-scale: These two characteristics make it possible to limit the zoom degree. If you set the maximum scaling to 2.0, the text can be increased twice.

CSS Units

CSS units express a length. This is used with widths, heights, distances, edges, etc. Syntactic information of units consists of a number and a unit. The number of 0 measured can be void. There are two kinds of units—absolute and relative.

Absolute Units

Absolute units are as follows:

- cm: Centimeter
- mm: Millimeter
- in: Inch
- px: Pixel
- pt: Dot
- pc: Pica

⚠ Typographic Information   Typographic units such as point and pica were adopted from the time of the paper printing. People defined the widths during the printout accurately. 1 Pica is 12 points, 1 point is 1/72 of an inch. In the today's world, screens have many sizes, widths, and dissolutions, so this type of information is senseless to a large extent.

The relationship between pixels (points on the screen) and an inch is fixed to 2.54 cm = a 96 resolution. With Windows, 1 inch = 1 pixels. Standard devices with normal dissolution supply a relationship of 1 equipment pixel to 1 pixel. Devices with high resolution, like printers or retina displays, supply n pixels to equipment pixel with = 1.

Table 4-6. *Medium Inquiry in an HTML Document*

System	Resolution	Device Pixel per Pixel
Mac	72	1
Windows	96	1
Mobile low	120	1
Mobile medium	160	2
Mobile high	240	2
Retina	300	3

If you want to find out the real dissolution, you can do so by using the instruction of the screen width and height, as well as the diagonal length of the screen. In the case of 4.65 inch smartphones with 1280x720 pixels, the result after the set of the Pythagoras would be:

```
sqrt(1280² x 720²) / 4.65 = 315.8
```

That is rounded to 316 inches. You then have to mark out the equipment, which usually means subtracting 320 dpi from it. Dividing by 96 (the resolution) results in a relationship of 1:3:33, which is rounded to 3 for the equipment pixel per pixel setting.

Absolute information should be used only if you know for sure how exactly the medium will display your page. That is more or less only possible for printers.

Recommendation   If you need an absolute unit, you should size to px if you're using the right screen. On a printer, you should use mm or pt.

Relative Units

Relative units use a certain starting point and are relative to other characteristics such a screen size and styles. The following units are available:

- em: Unit of the font size based on the height in pixels (1em is the size in pixels of a basic letter M)

- ex: Unit of the font size based on the height of the small letter x

- ch: Unit of the font size based on the width the number 0

- rem: Unit of the font size based on the width of the small letter m of the root element of the side (body)

- vw: Relative to 1% of the width of the viewport (with a 46cm screen width, 1vw = 0.46cm)

- vh: Relative to 1% of the height of the viewport

- vmin: Relative to 1% of the width of the narrow side of the viewport

- vmax: Relative to 1% of the width of the wider side of the viewport

- %: As a proportion of the original value

The em unit defines the size of the letter M as measure of the unit. This is not the case with CSS, the value is the browser standard, comparable to using the Times New Roman font. Which actual pixel value the browser uses is not clearly defined—by any means 12 pixels are not accurate and the known 16 pixels aren't guaranteed either.

Figure 4-6 shows that the standard font (here from Firefox) needs exactly 16 pixels for the letter M and that this corresponds to the instruction 16px. The red line is 16 pixels. As the font size in this image, 1em and 16px were adjusted and the same result was obtained.

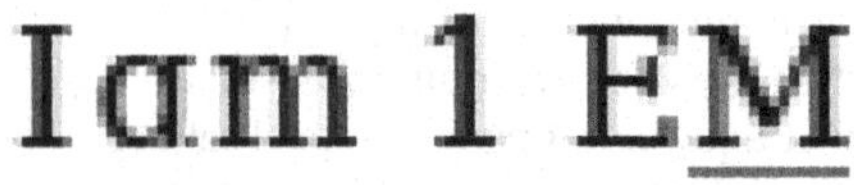

Iam 1 EM

Figure 4-6. *Measuring of the pixel unit, em*

Recommendation If you need a relative unit, use em or rem. The unit rem remains constant on the entire site; em however is valid for the current text in each case.

Index

© Jörg Krause 2016
J. Krause, *Introducing Web Development*, DOI 10.1007/978-1-4842-2499-1

Get the eBook for only $4.99!

Why limit yourself?

Now you can take the weightless companion with you wherever you go and access your content on your PC, phone, tablet, or reader.

Since you've purchased this print book, we are happy to offer you the eBook for just $4.99.

Convenient and fully searchable, the PDF version enables you to easily find and copy code—or perform examples by quickly toggling between instructions and applications.

To learn more, go to http://www.apress.com/us/shop/companion or contact support@apress.com.

Printed in the United States
By Bookmasters